D0820741

THE LIFE OF JEWS IN POLAND BEFORE THE HOLOCAUST

The Life of Jews in Poland before the Holocaust

A Memoir

BEN-ZION GOLD

University of Nebraska Press
Lincoln and London

Library of Congress Cataloging-
in-Publication Data
Gold, Ben-Zion.
The life of Jews in Poland before
the Holocaust: a memoir /
Ben-Zion Gold. p. cm.
ISBN-13: 978-0-8032-2222-9
(cloth : alkaline paper)
ISBN-10: 0-8032-2222-X
(cloth : alkaline paper)
1. Gold, Ben-Zion. 2. Jews—Poland
—Radom (Radom)—Biography.
3. Jews—Poland—Radom (Radom)
—Social conditions—20th century.
4. Radom (Radom, Poland)—
Biography. I. Title
DS135.P63G635 2007
305.892'4043841—dc22
[B] 2006014553

Set in Dante MT by Kim Essman.
Designed by A. Shahan.

I dedicate these memoirs to the memory of

My parents, Leibush Mendel and
Chana Chava Zyserman;
My sisters, Rayzel, Beila, and Esther,

Who were murdered by the Germans.

And my brother Pinchas, who
died before the war.

Contents

Introduction

There is an imbalance in the way we remember the Jews of Europe. Thousands of books have been written about the Holocaust, but only a few have been written about the life of Polish Jews before they were murdered. The Holocaust was undoubtedly the greatest tragedy in Jewish history, but it would be a mistake to treat it as a heritage. Our heritage is the way the Jews of Europe lived and what they created before the Holocaust. In fact, they left us a rich legacy in religious and secular literature, in Hasidic and klezmer music, in Yiddish folk songs, and in art. An indication of the vitality and richness of Jewish life in prewar Poland is the large number of newspapers and periodicals in Yiddish, Polish, and Hebrew that were published between the two wars. Despite poverty, that community produced more daily newspapers and periodicals than the larger and more affluent Jewish community of the United States. This cultural-religious heritage is awaiting redemption by the descendants of the murdered Jews of Europe. My memoirs, which describe the traditional life of my family and the community in which I grew up, are a small but significant segment of that heritage.

To this day, when I think about my family I remember the Shabbats and festivals at home, the *zmirot* (hymns) we sang at the Shabbat meals that uplifted us and turned these meals into memorable religious feasts. These memories have made life worth living in spite of their tragic deaths. These memories have given me the courage to raise a family in a world that I had experienced as deranged by the blood and agonies of our people.

At first I was writing these memoirs for my daughters, Hanna and Merav. I wanted to acquaint them with the heritage in which I had grown up and with the lives of their paternal grandparents, aunts, uncles, and cousins, whom they had never met because they were murdered by the Nazis. Later it occurred to me that this story of traditional life in prewar Poland might be of interest to other people as well.

All but the last three chapters of this book describe various aspects of my life in prewar Poland. Chapter 17, "Escape to Freedom," describes how I escaped from a convoy on the way to Dachau when I had reached the point of exhaustion bordering on death. It was a desperate act guided by a powerful will to live that I ascribe to my mother's love and to my traditional upbringing's emphasis on life. In chapter 18, "The Encounter," I describe how meeting people who remained ultra-orthodox made me aware of how much I had changed. Finally, chapter 19, "After Liberation," describes how I reconstructed my life after six years in ghettos and concentration camps. I feel that these three segments complete my description of how my home and community equipped me to deal with life even in the worst of circumstances.

The first sixteen chapters cover the period between 1927, when I was four, and 1940, when the Germans put us in a ghetto. In my effort to be faithful to the realities I describe, I discovered the uncanny way one's memory works. Often, remembering vividly just one kernel of the story so that I could visualize it led to the recovery of the whole story.

I wrote these memoirs over a period of twenty years. In the spring of 1983 I had a half-year sabbatical from my position as director of Harvard Hillel, and Millie Guberman, who knew of my intention to write, provided me with sufficient funds to spend that time in Jerusalem. I would like to take this opportunity to thank her for that generous assistance. When I returned, my job as director at Harvard Hillel again took up all of my time, and it was not until I retired in 1990 that I had time to resume writing. I was fortunate to have the longhand text of my memoirs written in Jerusalem, which served as the basis for this book.

Several people encouraged me and assisted in the writing of my memoirs. Foremost among them are my younger daughter, Merav, and my partner in life for the past twenty years, Nurit Lissovsky. Each read every part of the text and made sure that my story was coherent and readable. I also want to thank Deb Chasman, Illana Cohen, Emanuel Etkes, Irene Fairly, Richard Fine, and Ruth Anna Putnam, who read all or part of the book and made valuable suggestions.

THE LIFE OF JEWS
IN POLAND BEFORE
THE HOLOCAUST

1

Jewish Radom

My family lived in Radom, a city in central Poland about sixty-five miles south of Warsaw. In 1939 a third of Radom's eighty-five thousand inhabitants were Jews, and less than a third of these were Orthodox. Most of them were Hasidim, followers of Hasidic rebbes. They worshipped in *shtibls* (Hasidic places of prayer), of which there were about twenty. We prayed at the shtibl of Piaseczno Hasidism, where my father had studied. No rabbi officiated at our prayers. They were led by members of the congregation, all of whom knew the prayers, and some of them even had pleasant voices.

Four Hasidic leaders lived in Radom. One of them, Reb Yosele, was our neighbor. I got to know him well, and I describe our relationship later in these memoirs; the other three I knew only from afar. Reb Yankele had a son who was a Communist. Religious people felt sorry for Reb Yankele and pronounced the word "Communist" in a hushed voice as if it meant a criminal. Indeed, Communists were treated as criminals in Catholic Poland. Another Hasidic leader, Reb Moishele, was known as the *veibersher rebbe* (the women's rebbe) because he gladly received women, listened to their troubles, and gave them his blessings.

There were many heders in Radom where children from religious homes were educated. Some were elementary, where they learned to read Hebrew, while at others, staffed by several teachers, children also studied Bible and Talmud. I spent a year in the elementary heder that was located one block away from home, and I continued in a graded heder until I was twelve.

Jews lived alongside Poles throughout Radom, but there was also a predominantly Jewish section, the Vuel (in Polish, Walova), with the town synagogue, the Beit HaMidrash (house of study), several shtibls, and the *mikvah*, the public bath that was used also by women for ritual immersion after menstruation.

The Vuel and its side streets were dotted with shops serving Jewish needs: kosher butcher shops, Jewish bakeries, stores with a large selection of religious books and articles, and shops that sold Jewish garments and hats. Before Passover my father would take me to the Vuel to buy me a new hat. I wore what was called a "Jewish hat," which was black and looked like a baseball hat with a short cloth visor. The Vuel also had the largest and best Jewish delicatessen, which offered a variety of cold cuts, relishes, and beers. Yantche, its owner, presided over his establishment in a black yarmulka on his graying head and a white apron over his ample belly.

The Vuel also had one more attraction. My paternal cousins had a shop with a large selection of candies, nuts, raisins, and, of course, chocolates. The three Billander brothers were not married, and they apparently liked children. I would come away from their store laden with enough sweets to last me the whole week.

The Vuel was Jewish territory where I enjoyed feeling at home. I was fascinated by the vitality of the place, the variety of its shops, and the hustle and bustle of large numbers of Jews.

Once a week, on Friday afternoon, I would take a change of

underwear and a clean shirt and go to the mikvah. In our town the mikvah consisted of two large rooms. In the first room we undressed and washed the whole body with soap and water; then we would enter the second room, which had a large pool. In winter the pool was well heated. People entering it would sound a long "Ahhh" expressing both the heat and the pleasure. When they came out, their bodies were red and steaming. The mikvah was also a leveler: all of the people, whether ignorant or learned, rich or poor, were naked.

Our family lived on Zeromskiego Street, the main street of Radom, in a large apartment building with an inner courtyard. Both Jews and Poles lived in the building. Of the many Jews who lived there, only I and my friend Nahum Wolman wore traditional Jewish garments—the black capote and Jewish hat. No one troubled me about it, but I was aware of being different. I wore a "uniform," and at times I was proud of it, at times self-conscious. Being "marked," I avoided Polish neighborhoods because I was afraid of being attacked.

We shared our entry of the apartment building with five other families. Four of them were not religious. We met only on the stairway, and our contact with them was civil but not social. I not only remember them but have also dreamed about them. I was obviously curious about them. Our second-floor neighbor had a pretty daughter. She often sat on the balcony, and I would watch her from a distance. I didn't know her name and had never spoken with her. That was my first interest in a girl, and I was about nine or ten. Our paths didn't cross because I went to heder and then to a yeshiva, while she went to public school and then to the *gymnasium* (secular high school).

On Shabbat and holidays there was an important difference between the Vuel and the rest of the city, a difference that I would notice when I accompanied my father to services. Our path led from the center of the city, where we lived, to the Vuel. In our neighborhood there was no difference between its appearance on Shabbat and weekdays. In fact, I noticed that even some Jewish stores were open for business on Shabbat. When we got to the Vuel, the hustle and bustle that marked that area on weekdays was gone. Stores were closed and people were walking to services leisurely, dressed in their Shabbat best. At midday, when people ate their Shabbat meal, the streets were empty. The Vuel celebrated Shabbat and holidays.

Jewish life in Radom was organized by the *kehillah*, the Jewish community organization. Its leadership was elected by the members of the Jewish political parties. At one extreme were representatives chosen by the Agudah and Mizrahi. Both parties were religious, but Mizrahi was also Zionist. At the other extreme were members of the Bund, a secular Socialist party. In between were Zionist parties of various shadings. Yonah Zilberberg, the last president of the kehillah, was our neighbor.

Although I was too young to follow the activities of the kehillah, I was aware of its seamier side. In 1938 two representatives of the kehillah attempted to persuade my father to run for the office of president. My father refused, and I heard him say, "I shall always work for Jews but never with Jews." I was puzzled by his uncharacteristically harsh statement. At the time I simply assumed that he was referring to the intrigues among the political parties that were represented in the leadership of the kehillah. After the war I read in the *Radom Memorial Book* an article that described the deplorable methods Rabbi Kestenberg used to hold onto his position after he had been appointed by the governor to serve temporarily as rabbi. He resorted to libel to frighten away every candidate who was elected by the community and relied on strong-arm tactics of his few supporters in the kehillah. In the end he prevailed, but his was a Pyrrhic victory. Serious people like my father would have nothing to do with him.

Though the conflict over the rabbi and his reprehensible tactics cast a shadow over the kehillah, it didn't impair its functions. Most people continued to pay annual dues to the kehillah. These funds were used to pay the salaries of the rabbi and his assistants, the *shokhtim* (those who slaughtered animals), and other employees of the kehillah. These funds also financed the institutions that were sponsored by the kehillah: the Jewish hospital, the home for the aged, the home for orphans, the Talmud Torahs for children from poor homes, the shelter where itinerant beggars spent the night, and many other beneficial institutions and functions. Despite the problems that plagued the kehillah periodically, I wonder whether Jewish life in the United States wouldn't have been better off with a democratically organized kehillah instead of the philanthropies with a leadership that no one elected.

2

Home and Family

My father, Leibush Mendel Zyserman, born in Radom in 1895, was a religious Jew, well versed in traditional Jewish literature. He made a living from a wholesale beer and soft-drink business. Much of his free time was given to public service. He was a city councilman for twelve years, in which role he eloquently championed the welfare of his constituents and earned the respect of his colleagues for being a dedicated city father. I remember him working on the city budget into the wee hours of the morning. A devoutly religious Jew with a beard and wearing the traditional long coat, he was concerned about the welfare of all the citizens of Radom, Poles and Jews. Despite the prejudices rampant in Poland, he set before me the example of one humanity. His sense of humanity derived from the Bible and the Talmud, which were also the source of his Socialist leanings. Every morning at breakfast he read two papers: the *Jewish Daily*, the Yiddish paper of the ultra-Orthodox Agudah, and the *Worker*, the Polish Socialist paper.

My father's sense of responsibility to himself, to his family, and to society derived from his education. It was an education not of studying diverse subjects to acquire knowledge, but of an immersion in the study of Talmud to discover how to live, a subject that the sages discussed during five centuries. They also debated the role of learning and agreed that "Learning is great for it leads to [good] deeds." Considering that my father was a religious Jew who believed that the Talmud was a sacred work, it was bound to have a great influence on his life.

Before he was married, my father studied Talmud for about a decade. He was literally addicted to studying. He once told me that after he was married, when he no longer had time to study because he had to support his wife and his two sisters, he suffered from stomachaches. My father had a good memory, and he enjoyed peppering his conversations with apposite quotations from the Talmud.

Just as his knowledge was a guide to his ritual practices, so was it a guide for his relations with people. I remember walking with my father at a resort. It was Sunday morning, and I noticed that he was greeting the people who passed by him. At home he knew many people, and I was used to seeing him greet almost everyone he passed, but I couldn't imagine that he knew that many people in Otwock. I asked him, "Father, do you know all these people?" He stopped, looked at me with surprise, and said, "Don't you know that the Talmud bids us to greet everyone we encounter in the morning, including gentiles?" The rest of the way to the hotel I kept thinking about what he had said, and I never forgot it.

My mother, Chana Chava Kleiman, born in Dzialoszyce in 1894, was a sensitive, alert, and loving woman. Her main tasks were caring for the family and the household. She knew how to read Hebrew and Yiddish. On Shabbat she read the weekly *parashah* (Bible reading) in the Tzena Urena, the Torah in Yiddish with rabbinic comments read by women. During the summer and before Christmas, the busy seasons for beer, she helped my father in his business. My mother was a person of few but thoughtful words. She was eloquent in her devotion and love for us and remarkable in her ability to remain calm in difficult and even dire situations. Once, under the Germans, when she thought she was about to be killed, she took off her gold wedding ring and asked someone to deliver it to me. My parents loved and respected each other. My father, who was admired as a wise person, often sought her advice.

There were five children in our family. The oldest, Rayzel Chaya (b. 1917), graduated from public school and attended the Beis-Ya'acov religious school. She worked in my father's office. Rayzel got married in 1939, and she and her husband, Rachmiel, enjoyed several years of a loving relationship despite the harsh conditions of the German occupation. Beila Yehudith (b. 1919) received the same education as Rayzel and later worked in a bank. Beila was the intellectual of the family. She didn't hesitate to voice her independent critical views, for which we called her affectionately the "Bolshevik." Every moment of her free time—late into the night—Beila spent reading. Her intellectual curiosity was boundless and extended to reading books translated from various languages into Polish. I was born in 1923. I studied in a yeshiva, and during the German occupation I was active in the underground network of heders for Jewish children. My brother, Pinchas (Pinye) (b. 1925), was still in heder when he died in 1938 from appendicitis. Esther Rachel (b. 1927) was murdered in 1943 by the Germans.

Of my grandparents I knew only my mother's parents, Yonathan and Gitel Kleiman. They lived in Dzialoszyce, a small town in southwestern Poland, where he was a *shochet*. My father's parents had died before I was born.

The word *shochet* is usually translated "ritual slaughterer," but this is of little help in understanding the profession or the people who practiced it. The kosher meat business in Poland was in the hands of two diverse types: the *shokhtim*, those who slaughtered the animals, and the *katzavim*, the butchers who cut up and sold the meat. Since kosher slaughtering is governed by many laws, from the size of the knife and its sharpness to the examination of the lungs for traces of disease, the shochet had to be an expert in many laws. To receive certification he had to pass an examination in Talmud and Codes relevant to his subject. He also had to be a religious person who could be trusted to adhere to the prescribed laws even when pressured by the butcher to overlook some. The butcher who owned the animal stood to lose much. The butchers were generally ignorant but devout; many were physically strong, and they could be counted upon to defend fellow Jews when attacked.

Rabbis and shokhtim often came to their profession by default. They would start as young Talmudists of promise, and after marriage, when faced with the necessity of supporting a family, some would become rabbis and some would become shokhtim. Thus, the shochet generally was a *talmid chacham*, a learned man. Both the rabbis and the shokhtim were employees of the kehillah. The shochet's proper title was "Shochet Uvodek, slaughterer and examiner." Its abbreviation, "Shub," was a title that usually accompanied his name. People with the family name Shub are usually descendants of someone who had been a shochet.

Grandfather Yonathan was a gentle and affectionate person. Though I had seen him only several times, I became attached to him. During the past fifty years I have dreamed several times that I was traveling through towns and villages to visit my grandparents, and once I even got there. My mother also had brothers. I met one of them and remember him vaguely.

My paternal grandfather, Aaron, born in Radom, was a grain

merchant. At a time when most fathers hoped that their son would become a rabbi, he forbade my father to study parts of the Code that were essential to the examination for the rabbinate, telling him, "I'm afraid that in a pinch you might become a rabbi." What a pity—my father would have been a great rabbi. My grandfather's anticlericalism stemmed from the decline of the rabbinate during the nineteenth century. My grandfather died young, when my father was only nineteen, probably from heart trouble. I remember my father telling us that when he was about sixteen, he began to make himself a few cigarettes from my grandfather's tobacco before going off to study. When my grandfather was told by his doctor that he had to quit smoking, my father saw him pacing up and down the living room murmuring to himself, "What a terrible sin this [smoking] must be, I can't rid myself of it." That was enough for my father to give up smoking. That story was undoubtedly told for my benefit: my father had good reason to think that I had begun to smoke, but the story was not invented for that purpose. He wouldn't tell a lie even for a good cause.

I remember two episodes about my father that convey his sense of self and his sense of duty. Once, on the second night of Passover, he and I were returning home from the evening service. Suddenly my father felt that someone had kicked him, and he asked me to look for a policeman. I went looking for one and after a few minutes returned and told him that I hadn't found one. He was annoyed and accused me of not having looked long enough. I felt that he wasn't hurt, and I was eager to return home and to celebrate the Seder. We weren't far from our home, and I thought that when we got there he would have forgotten about the kick. But that is not what he did. At the next corner, the man was about to turn off the main street, but my father insisted that he go with him. We were near a police station, and that is where my father took him. The officer on duty knew my father and apologized to him, explaining that the man was drunk and that he would keep him there overnight. We then returned home and celebrated the Seder. My father must have been just as eager as I to get home, but he wasn't the kind to overlook a kick in the behind by a drunken Pole.

The second episode was about his sense of duty as a city councilman. My father had heard that the sanitation committee was planning to make a tour of bakeries. He joined the committee and then went to the Jewish bakeries to warn them of the inspection and asked them to prepare for it. About a week later he came home and was very upset. When we asked him what happened, he told us that the Jewish bakeries had done nothing to clean up their establishments. Sometime later, when he asked some of them why they hadn't done any cleaning, they replied, "We knew that you were coming and that we could rely on you to protect us."

3

My Father's Marriage and Business

My father was engaged to be married when he was twenty. He had been promised three years of Kest, a fellowship that is provided by the bride's parents to support the newly married couple while the husband continues to study. But that was not to be. After the engagement his father died and, being the oldest, he suddenly became the provider of the family, which consisted of his two younger sisters, his bride, and himself (his mother had died earlier). The trouble was that my grandfather had left no wealth and my father had no way to earn a living, no profession. In Poland religious Jews were not given a secular education, and he hadn't learned a trade, because that would have been beneath the dignity of a learned young man from a middle-class traditional family.

Fortunately, Mr. Kepler, a German grain merchant who supplied hops to breweries, knew and admired my grandfather, and he used his connections with the leading Warsaw brewery to arrange for my father to represent them in the city and district of Radom. That is how my father became a businessman. To make up for his lack of business experience, he took partners who were supposedly seasoned businessmen. Invariably they took advantage of him. After several such partnerships he concluded that he had already paid amply for his "apprenticeship" and took charge of his business. But these unfortunate experiences left him with a bad taste for business. I often heard him quote the verse, "The merchant has false scales, he loves to cheat" (Hosea 12:8). Throughout his life my father looked on his business activities as a necessity, since his real interests were learning and public service. He spent evenings reading medieval Jewish philosophers.

My father's business—his offices, warehouses, a bottling plant, and horse stables—was located on Kilinskiego Street, a five-minute walk from home. The beer was shipped from Warsaw by train in hundred-liter vats. A bottling machine drew the beer from the barrels, filling a dozen bottles at a time. When I was five or six my father's business appeared to me as a marvelous playground. I was fascinated by the immense barrels of beer, the large tubs where the empty bottles were washed, and the bottling machine that seemed like a steel animal feeding twelve pups at a time.

Most of all I was taken with the horses. It may seem strange that a child who was raised in a traditional home would develop a passion for horses. It was an instance of early assimilation. When I was a child we lived near the city's military headquarters. On Sunday mornings I would watch from the window the lineup of soldiers who were being marched to church led by mounted officers. I could think of nothing more dashing than an officer sitting erect on a sleek-skinned, well-groomed horse, wearing a well-fitted uniform with golden buttons, his leather boots adorned with silver spurs.

My father's horses were neither sleek nor handsome, but they were horses and within my reach. I took it into my head that I too would ride a horse. At noon the drivers who distributed the beer throughout the city returned for lunch. Before they sat down to eat, they would loosen some of the horses' belts and hang a bag of fodder around their neck while the horses remained hitched to the shaft. I watched the procedure and decided that this was my chance to get on top of a horse. I climbed up to the driver's seat, then carefully inched along the shaft until I reached the spot where one mounts a horse. As soon as I had gotten to the top, the horse reared up its hind legs and I came tumbling down. Being stubborn, I patiently tried again; this time the fall ended in a broken arm. That's when I finally got the message that the horse wasn't interested in my becoming an officer.

The beer was distributed to the restaurants and pubs of Radom in large, horse-drawn platforms; out-of-town deliveries were made overnight until my father purchased a truck. In the late 1920s motor vehicles were still rare in Poland, and a truck was something of a marvel, a horseless wagon. People generally traveled locally by horse and wagon, and for longer trips they took trains that linked all major cities in Poland. Our truck was an Italian Fiat, and I was proud that our family owned one. From time to time Moishe, our chauffeur, would take me for a short ride. It was a thrilling experience. I still remember the smell of the leather seats, the pungent odor of gasoline, and the fragrance of Moishe's cigarettes. Moishe wore the usual chauffeur's uniform, a leather jacket and leggings, but his manner was at odds with his uniform. He spoke hurriedly, like someone who is unsure of himself and afraid that his listener will lose patience. His gait was awkward: he shuffled his feet and moved his shoulders along as if he were dragging a load.

Later it turned out that the truck wasn't all that powerful, and it broke down often. Some said that it was poorly made, others argued that Moishe was a clumsy mechanic; both were probably right. In the end the truck was sold, a victim of the depression and Moishe's ineptness. But my affection for Moishe, tinged with a touch of pity, remained unaffected.

In the summer, the large barrels of beer were kept cold in a basement that was lined with thick slabs of ice that lasted through the summer. The ice business was then in the hands of the local prison. During February a caravan of wagons, loaded with rectangular ice slabs cut from the local lake, made its way to our plant. The drivers were prisoners in drab-green uniforms and caps without visors. As a child I was fascinated and frightened by them. They walked alongside the wagons at a measured pace holding a whip in their hands. Their faces, ruddy from the cold, seemed stern; they stared ahead of themselves as if to avoid contact with the people around them. At night I imagined their crimes and had nightmares.

I also remember another episode from that period. Across the fence from my father's business was an apple orchard, and it beckoned to me. One summer day, a friend and I spotted a breach in the fence just large enough for us to slip into the orchard. We were tearing away at an apple tree when suddenly someone sneaked up on us and caught us in the act. It so happened that the orchard belonged to Avrum Kaiser, the leader of the Radom underworld. He was a tall, handsome, and powerfully built man. He didn't beat us, he just took off our pants—we were still in short pants—and told us to follow him. He apparently knew who I was, because he led me, in my underwear, straight to my father's office. He gently pointed out to my mother that the fruit was still not ripe and could upset my stomach and that we had harmed the trees. He then handed my pants to her and left. I was mortified that I was caught, and even more so that I was paraded in my underwear. I would have preferred a beating to such disgrace.

4

My Religious Upbringing

I grew up during the late 1920s and early 1930s. In those years about three and a half million Jews lived in Poland, but less than a third of them were religious. Most young people of my generation abandoned religion for political or practical solutions to the dilemmas of Jewish existence. They were attracted to Zionism, to the Jewish Socialist Bund, or to Communism, the groups that were competing successfully for the allegiance of the younger generation. What sustained me was my religious upbringing. My family was cohesive: we loved and respected our parents. The practice of Judaism was an integral part of my family life; it was my culture. I felt different not only from Poles but also from secular Jews.

Our world was shaped by beliefs and practices that we acquired in early childhood mimetically from our parents before we were old enough to learn them from books. These practices, which determined the rhythm and tone of our lives, were derived from the Bible, the Talmud, and the Shulhan Aruch (the Code of Jewish law). We traversed Polish streets with our Jewish consciousness. Outside was just another workday, but in our hearts and minds, our homes and places of worship, it was Shabbat or Yom-Tov. Our daily, weekly, and annual religious practices influenced each other, creating a complex, fascinating, and multidimensional life that shaped our identity and gave direction and meaning to it.

Daily Life

First thing in the morning, even before getting out of bed, we recited *Modeh Ani*, thanking God for awakening alive, and the last thing before going to sleep, we finished our bedtime prayers declaring, "I place my spirit in His hand when I sleep and when I am awake." As a child I heard my father recite the prayers at dawn on winter mornings. While outside it was bluing and I was still wrapped in sleep, I heard him whisper his prayers, word by word, as if he were counting pearls. Our morning, afternoon, and evening prayers took about an hour. In the course of the day we recited about a hundred blessings. We lived in the presence of God, observing His commandments.

Our week was divided into Hol, six profane days of work, and Kodesh, the sacred time of Shabbat. Hol and Kodesh were bridged by anticipation of Shabbat and preparations for it, and also by the weekly Torah reading. Though the "Queen" or "Bride" visited us every week and we knew the hour and minute of her arrival, we looked forward to her arrival the way one waits for a dear guest. Thus, anticipation of Shabbat and longing for its arrival shed some luster and sanctity upon the week. Being engaged in the actual preparations drew the glow of Shabbat onto the weekdays and deepened our experience of Shabbat when it came. The same was true for the weekly Torah portion. The first part we read on Saturday at *minhah* (the late-afternoon service), then again on Monday and Thursday, and on Shabbat we read the whole parashah. These readings permeated our week with Torah, sacred scripture.

Preparations for Shabbat, including housecleaning, shopping, cooking, and baking, were performed by my mother, but they imbued all of us with a sense of the approach of Shabbat. After I had studied Talmud I discovered that some of the sages participated in the preparations of shopping and cooking. They also brought flowers in honor of Shabbat, a custom that was revived in Israel. In my religious environment the division of labor between the sexes had become rigid, and men were not welcome in the kitchen. As a child I loved watching my mother preparing the Shabbat food. I noticed their ingredients and absorbed their aroma. After the war, what I had observed, aided by my acute sense of smell, helped me to reconstruct my mother's gefilte fish, chicken soup, and chopped liver.

Actual preparations for Shabbat began on Thursday morning when my mother went to market to purchase the Shabbat fare: fish, chicken, meat, fruit, and vegetables. I grew up during the depression, and there were times when bread was scarce, but with my mother's ingenuity we welcomed the Shabbat Queen with a feast. The traditional fare of fish and meat, though smaller in size, were all the more festive by their presence on our Shabbat table. When the hard times passed, welcoming the Shabbat Queen became less heroic but more ample and joyous.

Friday was Erev Shabbat, the eve of Shabbat, and it had a rhythm of its own, as if Shabbat had expanded back into Friday. We went to heder only in the morning. At home we were greeted by a bouquet of Shabbat food flavors: the fragrance of freshly baked *challah* mingled with the pungent aroma of the gefilte fish, the soothing flavor of chicken soup, the lemon flavor of the dried fruit compote, and the vanilla fragrance of the cake. Friday lunch always included a little chopped liver or a piece of gefilte fish, a foretaste of Shabbat.

In winter my mother prepared a large pot of *chulent*, consisting of potatoes, rich meat, and spices. In that pot she also put a small pot of *kugel*, a side dish made of rice, prunes, and chicken fat; the pot was insulated with newspaper. The chulent with the kugel was delivered to the baker before Shabbat. The bakery's oven had been swept clean of embers, but the heat from baking bread during the whole week was still strong. In it the chulent simmered overnight until Shabbat noon, when we picked it up.

My mother was the first to usher in Shabbat. When she lit the Shabbat candles, she covered her face and recited silently a personal prayer for the welfare of the family in addition to the prescribed blessing. When she finished, we greeted her with "Good Shabbat." That is when Shabbat began. From here on, all weekday activities ceased until Saturday night.

After the candle lighting, my father, my brother Pinye, and I went across the yard to Reb Yosele's Beit HaMidrash for the Friday evening service. We began with Kabbalat Shabbat, the service of welcoming Shabbat that was created by the mystics of Safed in the sixteenth century. It consisted of six psalms and a hymn composed by Shlomo Alkabetz, a member of the Safed community. The hymn began with "Lekha Dodi," "Come, my friend, to greet the Bride let us welcome the Queen Shabbat," and it ended with the congregation facing the entrance singing "Come O Bride, come O Bride, Shabbat Queen." When we returned home the table was ready for the meal. The *challoth* that mother had baked were covered with a colorful cloth, and a bottle of wine with my father's silver kiddush cup were ready for the Shabbat feast to begin.

Shabbat was celebrated with three *seudoth* (festive meals), each with prayers and *zmirot* (hymns) of its own. The Friday night seudah began with singing "Shalom Aleichem"—welcoming the Shabbat angels, the angels of peace. My father recited a long prayer for the welfare of the family, after which we chanted

"Eishet Hail," an ode to the resourceful wife, taken from the last chapter of the Book of Proverbs. I always assumed it was meant for my mother. After these two hymns we sang a poem by Rabbi Isaac Luria, the great mystic of sixteenth-century Safed, and my father recited a selection from the Zohar, the medieval mystical commentary on the Bible. Both the poem and the Zohar were in Aramaic.

Several lines from that poem were overtly erotic: "Between right and left the Bride approaches in holy jewels and festive garments. Her husband embraces her in her foundation, gives her fulfillment, squeezes out his strength. Torment and cries are past. Now there are new faces and souls and spirits." As a child I didn't understand the poem, both because it was written in Aramaic and because I didn't know what it was describing. Later I discovered that, in reflection of the mystical union between God and the Shabbat Queen, husband and wife were required to engage in sexual union on Friday night. I wonder how my father, who was a rationalist, got involved in this mystical ritual. I tend to think that he simply continued the Hasidic ritual he grew up with. After these recitations, my father chanted the *kiddush* (the sanctification of the Shabbat) over a full cup of wine, and we all drank from it.

The seudah began with the ritual of washing the hands and was followed by the blessing of the challoth. The first course was gefilte fish. Eating fish and meat was part of the Shabbat seudah already in Talmudic times. Then came chicken soup with noodles. The main course was chicken, followed by a compote of stewed fruit, cake, and tea. Between the dishes, we sang zmirot. Some of the poems we sang were written by Dunash Ibn Labrat, Shlomoh Ibn Gabirol, Abraham Ibn Ezrah, and Yehudah Halevi, the great poets of medieval Spain. Others were written by medieval Ashkenazi poets, and some by sixteenth-century mystical poets who lived in Safed. The main theme of the zmirot was the joyous celebration of Shabbat. All of us had good voices and enjoyed singing, especially my father, who also had a good ear for music. We sang the zmirot to *nigunim* (melodies) composed at the courts of Hasidic leaders, especially by the rebbes of Modzhits, whose nigunim were favored by Jews of central Poland. During the winter, when it got dark in the late afternoon, we ate early and sang for about an hour.

Our Shabbat meals were festive but somewhat austere. My father wasn't given to small talk, and that set the tone of the meal. Our reverence and love for him was, by present-day standards, extraordinary. We were attuned to every nuance of his mood and spellbound by his commanding presence. That turned the meal into a blend of meal and ritual.

After the seudah, my father would study the Midrash, the rabbinic commentary on the *sidra* (the weekly Torah reading). Sometimes he would invite me to study Talmud with him. After reading a few sentences, he would begin to search the commentaries that are printed at the end of the volume without telling me what he was looking for. I suppose he was looking for answers to questions raised by the text. Had he told me, I probably couldn't have given him the answers, but I would have felt included.

On Saturday morning we got up an hour later than on weekdays. Adults, who were not supposed to eat before the morning prayers, drank tea; children under thirteen were served cake. We prayed at the shtibl of Piaseczno Hasidism, where my father had studied before he got married.

The second Shabbat seudah began around noon. The main course was the chulent that had simmered overnight in the baker's oven. The potatoes came out light brown, tender, and permeated with the taste of the meat and spices. These hot dishes were especially welcome in winter. In the summer the seudah began with a herring salad prepared with oil, pepper, onions, and tomatoes.

My father usually invited an *oirech* (a poor person) from among those who had lined up at the door of the Beit HaMidrash to join us for the meal. These were itinerant beggars, of whom there were, unfortunately, many in Poland. I was fascinated by these vagabonds who lived at the margin of our society, and their presence at our table added excitement and mystery to the celebration. At times, when they felt relaxed, they would recount some of their experiences. My father, for whom the Shabbat meal was a sacred feast, wasn't particularly interested in their tales, but he would listen respectfully. My mother, concerned that they were generally not well fed, would serve them generous portions. I remember an oirech with a gargantuan appetite. He ate three heaping portions of chulent, and he did it like a professional, slowly, as if he were carefully stocking the food inside him.

In our home Shabbat was sacred time. My father guarded against the intrusion of weekday activity or even conversation. Once Dr. Shenderowicz, a colleague from the city council, barged in during our Shabbat meal to tell father something, and I was surprised by how curt my father was with him. It was uncharacteristic of my father, and he was ruffled by it for a while afterward.

The nap that followed the noon meal was part of Shabbat pleasures. In the summer there was a long afternoon during which to study and to host guests. At minhah we read the first chapter of next week's Torah portion, creating a link between this Shabbat and the next. Then came *shalosh seudot*, the third prescribed feast of Shabbat. During the long days of the summer, shalosh seudot was a meal and we sang zmirot until it was dark. In the short days of winter, it came only a couple of hours after the noon meal and was a symbolic meal consisting of a bite of challah. When twilight came we had the somber feeling that Shabbat was coming to an end, but we prolonged it into the evening by singing zmirot. It was a time of mysterious quality, a precious finale to the holy day of rest and renewal.

At the end of Shabbat the many-colored braided Havdalah candle was lit and my father chanted the Havdalah, the prayer of separation, over a cup of wine. We sang "Hamavdil," a medieval poem about separation between the sacred and profane, and wished each other "A gute voch," a good week. The weekly cycle began all over again. But not really, because Saturday night was a half holiday called Motzaei Shabbat, the Departure of Shabbat, with a ritual of its own. In winter there was a long Motzaei Shabbat, and my father even managed to go to his business for a while. When he returned a fresh hot soup awaited him for the Melave-Malkah seudah, the feast of Seeing off the Queen. The theme of the zmirot for this meal was messianic, expressing longing and pleas for redemption.

The other activity that linked the profane and sacred parts of the week was the sidra. Two thousand years ago the five books of the Torah were divided into weekly portions to be read in the synagogue on Mondays and Thursdays and on Shabbat. At that time it was also decreed that each person over the age of thirteen review the sidra of the week by reading the Hebrew text twice and its Aramaic translation once. The reason for reading the Aramaic was that at that time the Jews of Palestine spoke Aramaic. Though we spoke Yiddish, we continued to review the sidra with the Aramaic translation the way it was done in antiquity, but with a reverse result: Aramaic, which once explained the Hebrew, was now explained by it. In heder we translated the sidra into Yiddish, and by reviewing it we learned Aramaic.

Torah reading was part of our educational and liturgical life. When I was six I learned several verses of the sidra each week in heder. By the time I was thirteen I, like all male adults, reviewed the whole sidra during the week. My mother read it in the Tzena Urena, a seventeenth-century Yiddish translation of the Torah interspersed with comments by Talmudic sages. On Shabbat the Torah portion was read publicly during the service. Thus, men and women, young and old, were familiar with the sidra of the week.

The weekly Torah reading brought us closer to the persons who appeared in it. We felt as if the patriarchs were our great-grandparents. We shared their joys and sorrows. Each year we experienced anew the drama of Joseph and his brothers. I felt ashamed that the fathers of the Jewish tribes were cruel toward their brother and mindless about causing grief to their father. Two weeks later when we read the sidra "Vayigash," with the story of their reconciliation, I was thrilled by Joseph's generosity toward his brothers. The "family" was whole again. The same sense of identification obtained with regard to other parts of the Torah. We were thrilled by the story of the Exodus from Egypt, awed by the revelation at Sinai, troubled by the golden calf, and saddened by the death of Moses. Repeated contact with the Torah also tended to concretize the more abstract parts of it. The Ten Commandments addressed us directly and emphatically: "*You* shall not murder." "*You* shall not steal." We were the "You" addressed by these commandments.

Two thousand years of weekly Torah reading had inspired the development of an extensive library of commentaries. Beginning with Midrash, whose authors were the sages of the Talmud, down to contemporary sermonic literature, all commentaries were written on the weekly sidra. This library includes Halachic, philosophical, mystical, moralistic, and Hasidic commentaries. All the commentators brought to the sidra the beliefs and dilemmas of their time, and together they reflect Jewish thought through the ages.

The Humash (the five books of Moses) that we used had the commentaries of Rashi from eleventh-century France; of Ibn Ezra from twelfth-century Spain; of Nahmanides, a near contemporary of Ibn Ezra from Barcelona; of Rashbam, a grandson of Rashi; and of Sforno from fifteenth-century Italy. These commentators, who lived at different times and places, referred to each other as if they were contemporaries at a round table. While reviewing the sidra, or during the Torah reading on Shabbat, we would glance at these commentaries. Having studied Humash with the commentary of Rashi in heder, one had acquired the basic vocabulary to read commentaries.

The extent to which the sidra permeated our lives can be gauged by the fact that the week was named after the sidra. Each sidra was named after a key word in its first sentence. Mentioning its name brought to mind the content of the sidra. That name was used to record important events in the life of the family as well as in dating correspondence. "The 2nd of the Sidra *Noah* 5699" translates into "Monday of the week when the Sidra of Noah was read in the year 5699," which corresponds to October 29, 1939. In sum, it is fair to say that the sidra of the week, like the preparations for Shabbat, served as a bridge between the six profane days of the week and the sacred time of Shabbat. Together they gave the week the cultural and religious depth that reinforced our daily life.

Holidays and Fasts

Like Shabbat, every holiday had a period of anticipation and preparation that enhanced our experience of it when it came. That was particularly true for Passover, a holiday that required specially prepared food, dishes, utensils, and a thorough cleaning of our home. That may also be why it was our most beloved holiday. Anticipation of Passover began as early as midwinter, when the story of the Exodus, which Passover celebrates, was read from the Torah during four consecutive weeks. Outside it was winter, but reading that story transported us in our imagination to Passover and spring.

The first preparations for Passover also began in midwinter. It was the time for putting up beets for borscht and rendering goose fat for Passover. In autumn geese were brought in from the field, kept in the barn, and fed well. By midwinter they had grown a heavy undercoat of down, become fat, and would fetch a good price. The rendering of goose fat was also memorable for the delicious hot goose cracklings that we ate with great relish. All other preparations were done between Purim and Passover.

I remember being taken along to *matzoh* baking. First a room was cleaned thoroughly to prepare a place for the matzoth. On the day of the baking we rose before dawn and went to the bakery. When we got there everyone was at work as if it were the middle of the day. To avoid the leavening of the dough, the work was done in assembly line. One person was mixing the water with the flour and making a cake, another rolled it out, a third poked holes in it, a fourth put it into the oven, and in no time there was a matzoh. While they were working we all sang Hallel, the psalms the Levites used to sing while the Paschal lamb was offered in Jerusalem when the Temple was still in existence.

After several hours we came home with a load of matzoth to last us for the eight days of the holiday. Locking the matzoth in the cleaned room was the first harbinger of the festival in our home. At the Seder we would point to the matzoth and declare, "This is the bread of poverty that our ancestors ate in the land of Egypt," and on this thin thread we reentered the drama of redemption.

Two weeks before the holiday, preparations became intensive. The house was given a thorough cleaning. My task, one that I enjoyed, was airing our library. For that purpose all the books were taken out of the bookcase and laid outside, volume by volume, their pages fluttering in the spring breeze. The evening before the Seder, my father conducted the prescribed search for *hametz*, in which I assisted him. That night, while the children were asleep, the Passover dishes were taken out of storage. In the morning when we got up, our home had changed: it was decorated by the colorful Passover dishes and wine cups.

The day before Passover we rose early and ate our bread breakfast near the door—the rest of the house had already been cleaned. When we finished eating we disposed of the crumbs outdoors and turned to the final preparations for the holiday. In addition to the symbolic foods that were placed on the Seder plate, my mother prepared a festive meal consisting of gefilte fish, chicken soup, roast turkey, and dessert.

In heder the weeks before Passover were devoted to preparations for the holiday. We studied the Haggadah and learned to chant the Four Questions. We also studied the Song of Songs with its traditional melody, the way it is chanted on the Shabbat during the week of Passover. That beautiful song about the love between a man and a woman was interpreted, following the Midrash, as a song of love between God and His chosen people, but we were intrigued by its plain meaning. Learning what we needed to know for Passover created a pre-holiday mood that led to a temporary "truce" in our usual conflict with the *melamed* (teacher). Our pleasure was enhanced by the knowledge that we were about to be liberated from heder for two weeks.

The cumulative effect of these repeated contacts with Passover throughout the year and the preparations for the holiday increased our anticipation so that the actual celebration of Passover became a fulfilling event. In our family, Passover was also enhanced by my father's spending the entire holiday at home. Because beer is fermented, it is prohibited on Passover, so my father could not go to his business.

The Seder in Our Home

For as long as I can remember, Leibl Shtekelman was our guest at the Passover Seder; the one time he was absent, the Seder was diminished. Leibl was a short man with a gray beard and a ruddy complexion; his mustache had the color of amber from heavy smoking and snuff. He walked briskly, a cane dangling from his arm, which gave him the nickname "Shtekelman"—cane man. Several days before Passover he delivered a small package of matzoh and a bottle of wine, foods required by law. Leibl felt that he should provide these on his own; the rest he ate with us.

We all had our seats at the Seder table. My father, wearing a *kittel* (white robe), reclined on a couch the way free people did in ancient times. Opposite him, at the wide side of the table, sat my mother surrounded by Rayzel and Beila. Esther, the baby, sat next to my father on the couch, and Pinye and I sat at the narrow end of the table. Leibl's place was semi-private; he sat opposite us, separated by a row of five silver candlesticks. My father, who had a very pleasant baritone, chanted the Haggadah, while the rest of us joined in the chorus, in which Leibel's rasping voice sounded like the base fiddle. From time to time the chanting was interrupted by comments.

During the meal Leibl regaled us with stories about Hasidic rebbes he had known. Leibl was a Kozhenitzer Hasid, that is, a follower of the Hasidic rebbe of Kozhenitz. He was proud to have known the old rebbe, the grandfather of the present one, and spoke about him with reverence. When Leibl told stories about the miracles performed by his rebbe, he would get excited and speak in half sentences that he completed with gestures and facial expressions. His face would become flushed, his eyebrows raised, his eyes tearing, and he would conclude with the exclamation, "Ho, ho, ho, that was some rebbe."

I once asked my mother, "How did Leibl become our permanent Passover guest?" She told me, "Many years ago, shortly after our marriage when Rayzel was still a baby, we had finished the Seder when there was a knock on the door. In came Leibl Shtekelman shouting defiantly, 'You already had your Seder, ha? Has it occurred to you to ask whether I had a Seder?'" Leibl had chosen the right door to knock on. Though my father was at that time in his mid-twenties, he was already a leader in the Orthodox community of Radom. Several years later he was elected to the city council. So instead of going to sleep, my parents set the table again and celebrated a Seder with Leibl. During the meal they found out that he had had an argument with his wife because, in his opinion, she had not been strict enough in her preparations for Passover. They quarreled, and instead of conducting the Seder, Leibl left home.

Leibl was proud and macho also in his religious observances. At the Seder when we all ate *maror* (bitter herbs), consisting of a piece of fresh horseradish root, Leibl took such a large piece that he nearly choked on it. His face turned red, his eyes were tearing. Long after all of us had finished, he was still chewing the root. The same happened with the first bite of matzoh. To fulfil the commandment of eating matzoh one had to eat a piece the size of a large olive, but Leibl would fill his mouth with so much matzoh that it took him a while to chew and swallow it. As a child I was both impressed and frightened that he might choke on it. Years later, I remember thinking that his eagerness to fulfill the *mitzvah* (commandment) at its most prevented him from fulfilling it at its best: the first bite of matzoh was supposed to be savored.

After the second Seder, Leibl disappeared; we wouldn't see him until sometime in the fall when he would suddenly turn up with a gift: old copper weights, an old watch, an old scale. From this I gathered that he was a dealer in used objects. On these occasions he would drink a hot glass of tea, smoke one of his cheap and pungent cigarettes, and leave. It was his way of saying "thank you."

The last time I saw Leibl was at our Seder in 1940. We had been under German occupation for eight months. The Germans had taken away my father's business and we were marked by armbands with a Star of David, making us easy prey for German violence. People who ventured out were never sure when or if they would return home. Some had already been murdered, some had been sent to concentration camps, but these were sporadic instances. We were still in our home, living off our savings, convinced that soon the war would be over.

This was the last Passover our family celebrated in prewar style. During the Seder we became so absorbed in the celebration that we forgot to be afraid. The story of slavery and liberation was uplifting, its message clear: just as we had survived to tell the story of the destruction of Pharaoh and the miraculous liberation of the Jews, so, with God's help, would we live to tell the story of the destruction of Hitler and his armies.

The Seder ended late. Leibl could no longer go home because there was a curfew limiting the hours when Jews were allowed to leave their homes. He had no choice but to spend the night with us. We offered him a bed but he refused, insisting that he would sleep on the floor. "The ground is my proper resting place," he muttered. He left in the morning, and we never saw him again.

Shavuoth

Six weeks after Passover we celebrated Shavuoth. In biblical times Shavuoth was an agricultural festival on which *bikkurim* (the first fruits) were offered in the Temple in gratitude for the harvest of grain. After the Temple was destroyed and many Jews went into exile, the sages of the Talmud provided the holiday with a new meaning. Having established that the date on which Shavuoth was celebrated was also the date of the revelation at Sinai, they changed the focus of the holiday. Ever since then Shavuoth celebrates the revelation at Sinai and is identified in our prayers as Zman Matan Torateinu, the time when our Torah was given.

In contrast to Passover, where the important part of the celebration, the Seder, is celebrated at home, the drama of Shavuoth takes place at the synagogue. The Torah reading for Shavuoth, chapters 19 and 20 of Exodus, vividly describes the Covenant of Sinai and the Ten Commandments. Read with scholarly detachment, they are chapters in the epic history of the Jewish people. When read on Shavuoth as part of the religious service, however, the same chapters become the occasion for reentering the experience they describe.

When I was a child, preparations for Shavuoth began a couple weeks before the holiday. We studied "Akdamut," a poem that is read directly before the Torah reading. This poem, written in Aramaic in the eleventh century, praises Israel for its devotion to the Covenant against all blandishments and threats of the gentile nations, and it describes the feast on fish, meat, and ancient wine that God has prepared for the righteous in the hereafter. The poem ends, "Exalted be the Lord through all eternity. He took delight in us and gave us his Torah." We also studied the Book of Ruth, which is read on Shavuoth. During my childhood, anticipating Shavuoth included looking forward to the special dairy foods, especially the cheesecake.

An important part of Shavuoth is the *tikkun* of Shavuoth night that was instituted by the mystics of Safed. It consists of reading excerpts from all the books of the Bible and the Talmud. When I was a yeshiva student we stayed up studying Talmud, which for us was the very essence of Torah.

The next morning, directly before the Torah reading, we chanted "Akdamut" and then read from the Torah: "On the third day, as morning dawned, there was thunder, and lightning, and a dense cloud on the mountain, and a very loud blast of the horn; and all of the people who were in the camp trembled. . . . Mount Sinai was all in smoke, for the Lord had come down upon it in fire; the smoke rose like the smoke of a kiln and the whole mountain trembled violently. The blare of the horn grew louder and louder. As Moses spoke, God answered him in thunder." Against this dramatic background Moses mediates the Covenant between God and the Children of Israel: "You have seen what I did to the Egyptians, how I bore you on eagles' wings and brought you to Me. Now then, if you will obey Me faithfully and keep My covenant, you shall be My treasured possession among all the peoples . . . and the people answered as one, saying, all that the Lord has spoken we shall do" (Exod. 19:16-19, 4-8). At this moment of heightened religious devotion, these words were not a story of what happened in the hoary past but a confirmation of a living Covenant. When we rose for the reading of the Ten Commandments we were again at Sinai experiencing Kabbalath Hatorah, receiving the Torah.

Another dimension of Shavuoth was reading the Book of Ruth. It is one of the most beautiful stories in world literature, a story of love, kindness, and devotion. Naomi, Ruth's mother-in-law, having lost her husband and two sons, is returning to Bethlehem. Orpah, one of her daughters-in-law, takes leave of her and returns to Moab. Naomi encourages Ruth also to return home, but Ruth replies: "Do not urge me to leave you, for wherever you go I will go; your people shall be my people, and your God my God."

Back in Bethlehem, during the harvest of wheat, Naomi directs Ruth to glean in the fields of Boaz, her wealthy relative. Impressed by Ruth's devotion to Naomi and by her humility, Boaz encourages her to glean in his fields. When at the conclusion of the harvest Boaz "ate and drank, and in a cheerful mood lay down beside the grain-pile," Ruth, encouraged by Naomi, showed up, "uncovered his feet and lay down. In the middle of the night, the man gave a start,—there was a woman lying at his feet! Who are you? He asked. And she replied, I am your handmaid Ruth. Spread your robe over your handmaid, for you are a redeeming kinsman. He exclaimed, Be blessed of the Lord, daughter! . . . I will do in your behalf whatever you ask." The story ends with the marriage of Boaz and Ruth. Oved, their firstborn, is the grandfather of David, the founder of the Judean royal dynasty.

That story also brought to our minds the sunny fields of Bethlehem that we, children in anti-Semitic Poland, longed for. Ruth's conversion was a moment of triumph for Jews, whom the dominant church despised. The fact that David, Ruth's grandson, was also the progenitor of the Messiah took the story one step further to the redemption of all Jews from the yoke of the goyim, the gentile nations. Together, the Covenant of the Torah reading and the pastoral of Ruth, along with the special foods and decorations, provided a rich fare of experiences that we treasured, a veritable feast for the imagination.

Tishah b'Av

Several weeks after Shavuoth we entered a period of mourning for the destruction of the Temple. It began with the fast of the Seventeenth of Tamuz, the day the Romans breached the walls of Jerusalem, and was followed by three weeks of mourning that culminated in the fast of Tishah b'Av—the Ninth of Av—the day the Temple was destroyed. This period of mourning, which corresponded to mid-July, was the most beautiful time of midsummer when fruit was ripening. As a child I was more attuned to the blessings of summer than to the distant events we were mourning.

During the nine days that preceded the fast, when the eating of meat was forbidden, I enjoyed my mother's delicious fruit soups. Even the mourning of Tishah b'Av was relieved by the playfulness of the children. During the reading of the Book of Lamentations, when the adults were sitting on the ground like mourners, the children tried to distract them by throwing burrs at their beards. Trying to extract the burs distracted them from the heavy mood. When I was about eleven and was allowed to fast until noon, I enjoyed smoking a cigarette that compensated for my fasting.

Yamim Noraim

The High Holidays, which we called Yamim Noraim (the Days of Awe), do not celebrate events in our history; instead, they focus on ourselves, on our relationships with other people and with God. Preparations for Yamim Noraim began on the first day of Elul, the month before Rosh Hashanah, with the blast of the *shofar* (ram's horn) that was sounded daily at the end of the morning service until the holiday. That jarring sound of the shofar startled us unto the awareness that the season of Teshuvah, or Repentance, had begun. Our response to that call consisted not only of greater care in our religious devotions but also affected our behavior; people behaved more gently with each other.

An important element in the preparations for the Days of Awe were the *selihoth* (prayers for divine pardon) that were recited beginning at midnight on Saturday before Rosh Hashanah. Thereafter these prayers were recited before dawn. Getting up for selihoth when it was still dark conveyed to me the solemnity of the event, and I was proud to be included. The selihot service before Rosh Hashanah also took place at midnight. It was called "Zkhor Brith" (Remember the Covenant), after the prayer in which we plead that in judging us God remember the covenant with Abraham and the binding of Isaac. In these prayers we acknowledge our human failings and appeal for divine mercy.

Like all holidays, Rosh Hashanah was divided between celebration at home and at synagogue, except that Rosh Hashanah services lasted a major part of the day, ending at two in the afternoon. As a child I liked going to services with my father, and I enjoyed the snack mother sent along, but I resented the long hours spent in prayer. At home my mother had prepared a feast with tasty food and delicious cakes, while my father and I spent most of the time at services.

The ritual at home resembled the Passover Seder. After kiddush we ate foods with symbolic significance. There was the apple with honey accompanied by the wish that it be a good and sweet year, then the circles of carrots, sautéed in chicken fat and honey, that looked like golden coins. We ate them wishing that our merits increase. The connection between carrots and increase is based on the similarity in Yiddish between the sound of the word for carrots (*meirin*) and the word for increase (*mehrin*).

When I was old enough to understand the Rosh Hashanah prayers I sensed how awesome the event we celebrated was. The morning service began with the prayer leader's loud exclamation, "Hamelekh," the King, as if he were announcing His arrival. The words that follow, "who sits on a high and exulted throne," suggest majesty and judgment, a theme that is emphasized in the liturgical poems of the service. Reciting these prayers that acclaim God's kingship, acknowledge His justice, and plead for His mercy instilled awe and pride in me.

In the shtibl where my father attended the holiday services, the prayer leader on this occasion was Chayimel, a short man with a loud but screeching voice. His shout of "Hamelekh" was an affront to majesty. I remember asking my father to let me go to the town synagogue where the town cantor was chanting the service, and my father responded, "That is a performance." I felt that it was indeed a good one. To this day I can't understand why my father, who had a pleasant and melodic voice, was satisfied with Chayimel's "performance."

The cumulative impact of the shofar every morning for a whole month, the penitential prayers during Slichoth services at dawn and midnight, and the two days of Rosh Hashanah suffused with prayers that celebrated God's sovereignty, His concern for the world He created, particularly for humanity that bore His imprint, and His promise of future redemption, gave us a sense of being at the center of a cosmic drama. I remember standing next to my father in his white robe and *tallith* (prayer shawl), the Ark open and the cantor leading us in the coronation poem to which we responded shouting the refrain, "Adonai Melekh, Adonai Malakh" ("The Lord is King, was King, and shall forever be King").

Rosh Hashanah as the Yom Hadin, the Day of Judgment, was described dramatically in the medieval poem "Untaneh Tokef," in which the poet, using images from the Talmud, describes the heavenly trail: "The great Shofar is sounded, and a still small voice is heard, the angels, quaking with fear, declare: 'The day of judgment is here.'" After reciting a list of decisions affecting life that are made on Rosh Hashanah but sealed on Yom Kippur, the whole congregation joins the prayer leader, shouting, "But repentance, prayer, and charity cancel the stern decree."

The ten days of Repentance that began with Rosh Hashanah ended on Yom Kippur. It was a short period that was dominated by self-searching and burdened by concern for our fate. It was also interrupted by diverting activities. One of them was Kapparoth (Atonements), a ritual in which one's sins are passed on to a chicken, a rooster, or even a fish, which is offered as a substitute for oneself.

The day before Yom Kippur was a half holiday. The tone was hushed. People asked each other for pardon of unwitting offenses. It was also a day in which eating was enjoined. The *seudah hamafseket* (the meal before the fast) was like a holiday meal consisting of several courses. My mother's candle lighting took longer than on Shabbat. She prayed silently for the welfare of her family; her prayer was personal and direct, and when she finished her face was wet with tears.

We went to services before sunset. When we got there, people in stocking feet, robed in white kittels, reminiscent of shrouds, and wrapped in the tallith, were reading the Tefillah Zakah, a prayer that provided us with the words to express our feelings of regret for having failed to live up to our beliefs.

Our service followed the Hasidic ritual. Before the chanting of Kol Nidrei, the Ark was opened and the people rose. Torah scrolls were taken out of the Ark and were carried around for people to kiss. Then the prayer leader chanted the verse from Psalms, "Or Zarua Latzadik" ("Light is sown for the righteous, Joy for the upright"). And the people responded. The verse was repeated several times. With each round the chant rose resoundingly and enveloped us, providing an effective beginning of our

Yom Kippur prayers. The solemnity of Yom Kippur ended with Neilah, its final service. Though tired from fasting and long prayers, people were relieved and cheerful, confident that their merciful Father in Heaven accepted their prayers. The day after Yom Kippur they turned to preparing their *sukkahs* (wooden booths) to celebrate the festival of Joy.

Sukkoth

Sukkoth, the third annual festival, celebrated in the autumn, was called Zman Simhateinu (the Time of Our Rejoicing). We celebrated it by eating in the sukkah and blessing daily the *lulav* (palm branch) and *ethrog* (citron fruit) as prescribed in the Bible. In the following episode I describe my experience of this festival in my childhood.

Sukkoth eve: The holiday is about to begin; my sisters have finished decorating the sukkah, and I walk around like the proud owner of a castle. Right after Rosh Hashanah, Rayzel and Beila, my two older sisters, began to prepare decorations for the sukkah. As soon as they came home from school they would sit down to work, cutting up shining colored paper and folding it tightly into links to make a chain. When they put links together they took care to match the colors so that the chain looked like a rainbow.

The sukkah itself was built later. The day after Yom Kippur, my father, assisted by several neighbors, took the carefully matched sukkah parts out of storage and joined them with nails. My job was to hand over the nails as they were needed. When the walls were up, we spread a roof of deep green reeds freshly cut at the riverbanks. There was something special about our sukkah: it had a glass window, small but real. When you looked in there was just enough light to see the colorful chains against the green roof, and it was beautiful.

A tree house in the summer is exciting, but how can you compare a tree house built by kids to a sukkah built by my father, who was always busy! A tree house is a children's game, but a sukkah, that's something different. All the grown-ups ate in it for eight days, and some even slept in it; it was like the whole family was playing house. My mother prepared the best foods, and guests were invited. Sukkoth was easily the happiest holiday of the year. When the holiday began, the table in the sukkah was covered with a sparkling white tablecloth, and on it were the glittering silver kiddush cups, bottles of wine, shining brown challahs, and the beautiful holiday dishes. I could barely wait until evening.

The first night in the sukkah was like a party and a holiday together. Dressed up for the holiday, we received our neighbors who didn't have a sukkah of their own, and before we sat down to eat we invited the *ushpizin* (invisible guests) from long ago—Abraham, Isaac, Jacob, Moses, Aaron, David, and Solomon—one for each day of Sukkoth. You remember how exciting it is to watch for Elijah at the Passover Seder? Well, on Sukkoth there are seven invisible guests, and imagine, I would be free from heder for nine days, nine whole days. I walked around as if in a beautiful dream.

Before bathing and dressing I went to take a final look at the sukkah, and I noticed a tall young man of about eighteen in the courtyard. I went over to say hello and found out that he was a student in the famous Slobodka yeshiva in Lithuania. He told me that he was in trouble. He had spent the High Holidays with his parents in a little town not far from our city, and on the way back someone had stolen his suitcase with all of his belongings. He didn't even have a clean shirt for the holiday.

As I was listening my eyes took in his handsome, olive-complexioned face framed by the blush of a black beard and his penetrating, coal-black eyes. I had a strong desire to help him. I knew that my mother had prepared a clean shirt and underwear for my father. Quietly I went into the house, took the shirt, wrapped it in a newspaper, went out into the courtyard, and gave it to the young man. He took the shirt, thanked me, and said, "I would like to tell you something important that I learned in the yeshiva. Our sages of the Talmud said, if someone tells you, 'I have worked hard and learned nothing,' do not believe. If he says, 'I did not but I learned,' do not believe. If he says, 'I worked and found out,' believe him." After that he blessed me and left.

It didn't take long for my mother to discover that the shirt was missing. When I told her what I had done, she scolded me mildly, then gave me a reassuring hug, but my sisters made fun of me. I had just turned nine, and I had been studying Talmud for a year and was very proud of it. Acting like a young Talmudist, I repressed my natural playfulness and observed every law to its last detail. My sisters felt that I was becoming too pious. Inside I knew I had done the right thing; my father had so many white shirts, and that nice young man didn't even have one for the holiday.

That evening as we entered the sukkah, my father, standing at the entrance, recited in Aramaic, "Bematu minach Avraham Ushpizi Ilaee," inviting Abraham the patriarch to be our guest of honor on the first day of Sukkoth. As I listened to my father, that young man's face appeared before my eyes: his olive complexion, blue-black beard, and glittering black eyes. It suddenly occurred to me that he was none other than the prophet Elijah, who often came disguised as a poor man. A shiver went through my whole body. I never told this to anyone, not even to my father. True, he was religious, but I knew he was a rationalist. He didn't believe in the miracles of Hasidic rabbis.

My religious upbringing required a traditional education. I needed to know the laws and customs we observed; the Siddur (the traditional prayer book), which had the prayers I recited daily; the Torah, which we read weekly; and the Talmud, which was the basis of our religious life. Heder education, despite its shortcomings, provided the education that a child living within the traditional daily, weekly, and annual cycle needed. That is the simple but true explanation for why my painful experiences in heder (which I will discuss shortly) did not prevent me from acquiring the religious education I needed. My classmates who didn't come from traditional homes got little out of heder. What they learned there was not linked to life and was too meager to launch them on an independent course of traditional Jewish living, especially when the street was also against it. In addition to my home I also received encouragement from the people who visited our home, from the people I met at the shtibl where we prayed on Shabbat, and from the people I met in the Beit HaMidrash of Reb Yosele, the Hasidic rebbe who was our neighbor, where we prayed on Friday nights and holiday evenings.

Our religious beliefs were shaped by the Siddur and the Torah. The two were in dialogue: in the Torah God was addressing us, and in the Siddur we were speaking to God. For example, twice daily before reading the Shma, a passage from the Torah in which we are commanded to love God and observe His commandments, we declare, "You have loved us and therefore gave us a Torah and Commandments." We spoke about divine revelation as an act of love. This dialogue between the Siddur and the Torah shaped our religious life. Our beliefs were not derived from a catechism or a set of beliefs imparted by parents or teachers; instead, they were shaped by the Torah and the Siddur, which were also the source of our parents' beliefs. As soon as I had learned to read the prayers, my father gave me a small Siddur of my own. I treasured that Siddur, and I still remember the golden letters on its navy blue cover. When people comment on my fluency in Hebrew, I tell them that I have spoken Hebrew since I was a child. That was true because I indeed spoke to God in Hebrew. Though I cannot recall what I believed in my childhood, knowing the sources that shaped my beliefs enables me to reconstruct them. In fact, the Siddur and the Torah—the books I used during my childhood and youth—have provided continuity amidst the changes and disruptions caused by the war and the concentration camps.

5

Heder

In religious homes, children were taught short prayers and blessings over food as soon as they were able to speak. When they reached the age of five, boys went to heder, the elementary religious school. Heder education began with learning the Hebrew alphabet and reading and translating the Siddur. It continued with the study of Humash (the five books of Moses), the commentary of Rashi, and beginning Talmud. Before every holiday we learned its special prayers and practices.

The heder usually belonged to the melamed and met in his home. The cost of heder education varied according to the reputation of the melamed, and it was paid by the parents. Many parents would go beyond their means to send their sons to a good heder. Children from poor homes went to the Talmud Torah, a heder that was supported by the community. In small towns the child's family knew the melamed: they prayed at the same synagogue and met at social and communal events. In large cities the melamed would visit the parents of prospective pupils and would keep in touch with them throughout the year.

In my time the heder had come under the regulations of the new Polish government. For public health reasons, the government prohibited locating the heder in a private home. To defray the costs of rent, several melamdim would rent a larger space and establish a graded heder. When that happened, relations between the melamed, his pupils, and their parents became less personal.

My parents were particularly attached to me because I was their first son; two sons before me had died in infancy. When I was five, instead of sending me to heder, they hired a tutor who came daily to instruct me at home. Being an occasional tutor, he must have been very poor. He was tall and lean with a black beard, a gaunt face, and melancholy black eyes. I don't remember ever hearing him speak. He had an alphabet sheet with large letters and vowels, and he used a wooden pointer to guide me. I was a playful child, and his silence was hard on me. To liven up the session I would occasionally snatch the pointer from between his fingers. He didn't appreciate my attempt at play and showed his displeasure with a pained look on his sad face, turning my playfulness into mischief.

Heder used to begin with a ceremony. The child was brought in his father's arms wrapped in a tallith. The melamed would take the child into his lap and, to associate the study of Torah with sweetness, would put before him an alphabet treated with honey. The child was taught some of the letters, and then he was invited to lick the honey. In some heders a shower of candy would come down on the child. When I started heder there was no sweetening ritual. When I was six my father walked me to heder on the first Sunday after Passover. The melamed received him with deference and promised to take good care of me. After my father left I was assigned a seat alongside the other "scholars." The change was abrupt and painful.

We sat on benches before narrow desks on which we placed our alphabets. As I was sitting there, being drilled on the alphabet that I had already learned at home, I became more and more angry. I would have cried, but I was too proud for that. By the time I was allowed to go home I was so enraged at my father for having abandoned me and so exhilarated at being released that I tore up my notebook, tossed the pieces up in the air, and shouted, "Look, children, it's snowing, it's snowing."

When I came home I told my mother that under no circumstances would I ever return to heder. My mother tried her best to calm me, explaining how she had hoped that I would someday become a talmid chacham (a scholar) and what a disgrace it would be if I were to grow up to be an ignorant man. Her sweet reason was of no avail; I remained adamant in my refusal until my father came home. My mother informed him of my rebellion, they whispered for a few minutes, and then he announced sternly, "All right, if you will not go to heder I'll apprentice you to a shoemaker." That did it. To my mind's eye came Yankel the shoemaker, who lived with his wife and three children in a basement apartment in our building. His hands and even his face were always soiled from working with shoemaker's tar, his clothes dirty and tattered. I decided that becoming a shoemaker was a fate worse than going to heder. I submitted to heder the way one accepts the inevitable, but I never made peace with it.

Heder changed my life abruptly. For five years I was a little prince at home, but in the sixth year I became one of fifteen waifs in a dreary heder in the care of a gloomy melamed. If that wasn't enough, when I become a student my father's attitude toward me changed. Now I had to earn the praise that he previously lavished on me freely. There were things I had to learn, things I had to practice. I was already in training for the performance of the commandments, on my way to becoming an observant Jew. Instead of his enabling approval I received his criticism. In no time this led to a rebelliousness that expressed itself in devious ways: playing tricks on my teachers, finding ways of staying home or playing hooky, and helping myself to change from my father's pockets.

Most melamdim had no professional training other than a rudimentary knowledge of the subject they were teaching. Their reliance on repetition and punishment led to an adversarial relationship between teacher and student. When we studied verses in the Torah, we translated each word separately: *vayomer* ("and he said"), *el* ("to"), *Moshe* ("Moses"). That was boring. While we were repeating the lesson the melamed paced up and down the room like a prison warden, holding a ruler ready to slap the hands of those who were caught guilty of inattention or unruliness. Once we staged a rebellion. The boy whom the melamed was going to hit got up and began to run around the benches, and the whole class ran after him. We ran in circles and prevented the melamed from striking him.

My first Talmud teacher read with us a passage dealing with the case of a person who stumbled over a pitcher that someone had placed in a public space. He didn't explain the complexity of the case, but he wanted us to decide whether the one who broke the pitcher had to pay for it. There were two of us in his class, about eight years old, and we couldn't make up our minds. Under pressure we came up with a new word, *pucha*, made up from the first half of the Hebrew *patur*, meaning "exempt," and *chayav*, meaning "guilty." The poor man was so high-strung that he began to tremble and stutter. It has since occurred to me that his nerves may have been frayed by malnutrition.

There was one exception, Reb Hendel Rosenberg, who used his imagination and eloquence to interest us in the study of the Bible. He addressed us as intelligent children, and we responded. The other melamdim turned the traditional sources of Judaism into drudgery. The results were that children who came from homes that lived by the tradition had contempt for heder, and those who came from homes where tradition was neglected came away from heder with contempt for the tradition.

Government regulations required that we study the Polish language, history, and arithmetic several hours a week. Our teachers of secular subjects were either assimilated Jews or Christians. They usually treated us well, and the stories and poems we read with them were interesting. The difference between the secular teachers and the melamdim was not lost on us. It may seem strange that a school dedicated to the preservation of a traditional way of life would provide its impressionable students with attractive alternative models. But little could have been done about it. Secular studies were discouraged in the traditional community, and no traditional Jews were licensed to teach secular subjects. The community was unprepared to cope with the regulations of the new Polish government.

The ineptness of the melamdim and their tendency to resort to punishment created an unpleasant atmosphere in heder. It is therefore not surprising that I periodically played hooky. I would get up in the morning and complain that I wasn't feeling well. I was unusually thin—skin and bones—and it was enough for me to complain of a stomachache and my mother would let me stay at home. I don't think I succeeded in fooling her. She was too smart for that; I suspect she tacitly collaborated with me. Once I overdid it and complained for several days in a row that I wasn't feeling well. My mother began to think that perhaps something was really wrong with me and took me to see a doctor. After examining me he declared, "May he always be as well as he is now." This put an end to my excuses for a while. But I found other ways to avoid the burden of heder.

In the winter the day seemed even longer than it was. We went to heder from eight in the morning till six in the evening with an hour break for lunch. The dark afternoons gave us the feeling of studying day and night. Soon I discovered a way to shorten the heder day. I would return from lunch early and cut the electric wires at an inaccessible spot. When it got dark all of us would be sent home. In winter that meant at least two hours ahead of time. I knew that what I did was illegal, and I would sit there barely able to contain my excitement. I must have felt the way juvenile delinquents feel after their first trespass. My fellow students never knew who their benefactor was. I don't remember what made me stop—most likely it was the fear of being discovered and the disgrace that would follow. I was a good student and the son of a distinguished family. When I think of it, I'm still surprised that I never bragged about it to anyone. My best friend at that time, Nahum Wolman, would have been shocked by my revelation.

At the same time that I was committing these offenses, I continued to be a devout and orderly child. No one except my father would have suspected me of such wild behavior. As for myself, what I did was a combination of childish bravado and resentment for being cooped up in heder. I had a quick grasp and a good memory; it was enough for me to hear the melamed translate and explain the Bible lesson once. But to make sure that all of the students knew the lesson we repeated it over and over again throughout the week, and I was bored most of the time. I suspect that my errant behavior was also directed against my father. Heder was a turning point in our relationship. Before heder his love for me was unconditional; when I became a student he became judgmental. Traditional parents tended to express their love through their criticism.

When I was about ten, Zvi Kaner and I became friends. His father had died, and his mother, a consummate businesswoman, spent all of her time running their leather goods business, leaving Zvi and his younger brother to take care of themselves. They lived in a sizable apartment above the business. Whenever I visited them they were alone making sandwiches and tea. They were self-confident and relaxed. It was fun to be with them. In late spring, a week after Shavuoth, Zvi told me that he was going to skip heder the next week and was thinking of going to the circus. I was already studying Talmud and was made to feel that I should behave as befitting a young Talmudist, which didn't include going to a circus and many other things that a boy of my age would enjoy. I liked the idea of going to the circus, and, though I had never played hooky for a whole week, I felt that if Zvi could do it, so could I. Besides, it's more pleasant to play hooky in company. I made up my mind to go with Zvi.

On Sunday morning I took some money from my sister Rayzel's coat pocket and left home with lunch and books as if I were going to heder. When I met Zvi we decided to go to a garden on the outskirts of town where we would avoid meeting people who might know us. The gardener was busy tending his young tomato plants, setting them out symmetrically over a large field. When I complimented him on his garden, he took the time to tell me how to grow tomatoes. In the course of our conversation he also told me that when he had graduated from the school of agronomy, some of his Jewish classmates went to Palestine. Ten years later they were owners of orange groves, whereas he was still renting his garden.

I remember this conversation because it was the first time I spoke with an educated Pole and he treated me seriously, as if I were a grown-up. There was yet another reason: for several years we had been spending summers in the country (in Yedlnia, a village not far from Radom), and I was fascinated by the fruit and vegetable garden at the cottage, by the endless woods full of blackberries, by the small but fragrant wild strawberries, and by a large variety of mushrooms. When I met the gardener I was but ten days away from this beautiful and charmed world of nature.

That evening, as I approached home, I was overcome by fear and remorse. I was afraid that my parents had discovered my delinquency, and I made up my mind not to do it again. But when I saw that they didn't have the slightest suspicion, I was encouraged to continue. And so I spent the last week of heder becoming acquainted with outlying parts of my city. The circus was fascinating, full of magic and excitement—performing lions, dancing elephants, beautiful girls swinging on trapezes and riding slick horses. Friday noon the ordeal with its thrills was over. I returned home from my wanderings, knowing that on Sunday, after half a day in heder, my mother and the younger children—Esther, Pinye, and myself—would go off to the country for the summer. I had carried off my longest stint of playing hooky and was relieved that it was over. But was it?

Sunday morning, as I was getting ready for heder, my father suggested that he would like to accompany me. That sounded strange; he had never done so before, and I had the feeling that something was wrong. I tried to dissuade him, but he persisted and we left home together. The walk to heder that morning seemed to take a long time. We walked side by side silently. There was something eerie about it. My father was usually direct. Why would he suddenly be playing a cat-and-mouse game with me? I remember hoping against hope that in the end he would give up before we reached heder. I simply couldn't believe that he knew what I had done the previous week and kept silent.

When we arrived, my father walked me to my class. On the threshold we stopped, he looked at me, his handsome face distorted by pain and anger, and he gave me a resounding slap in the face. Then he turned to Reb Hendel and said: "Ben-Zion is not going away this summer. He has had his vacation already."

That my father, a man of exquisite manners, would behave in a way that was so incongruous for him shows the degree of pain and concern I had caused him. But at that moment this was the last thing on my mind. As soon as he left, I went over to my seat and put my head on the desk. I was in agony: I, a leader in my class, slapped before all of them, in the presence of my favorite teacher. How degrading! How terrible! For a while I felt sorry for myself. Then my thoughts moved from anguish to anger. Did he have to punish me publicly? Did he have to shame me before my whole class? What hurt most was the thought of being denied what I cherished most: going away to the country. The mere thought of it was unbearable. As I sat there with my head on the desk I began to search for a way out of this preposterous situation, and soon I came up with a scheme. While I was in heder my mother had left for Yedlnia with Pinye and Esther. I was determined to get there. But how?

In late spring the government, seeking to encourage railway travel, had begun a policy of charging only ten cents for a child under thirteen when accompanied by an adult. At the lunch break, instead of going home, I asked my friend Nahum to tell my father that I had gone to the country, and I went directly to the railway station. Before long I met a friend of the family, and he asked me what I was doing at the station. I explained that I was on my way to our summer place but had forgotten the money for the ticket, and he immediately invited me to go along on his ticket.

I arrived in Yedlnia at sunset. As I stood on the railway platform trying to decide how to get to our cottage, I noticed my mother approaching the station. She was carrying a pot of fresh milk and had decided to stop by the station. I rather suspect that, knowing me, she expected I would show up. We walked home and she asked no questions. During the whole week I worried about what would happen when my father came for Shabbat. When he came he behaved as though nothing had happened. Later I discovered that my friend Nahum had forgotten to tell my father where I had gone. When it got dark my father and my sister Beila became worried and went out looking for me. When they came to Nahum's house he was already asleep. Finally, after searching for a while they decided to return to Nahum. When they woke him up he exclaimed, "Oh! I forgot to tell you! Ben-Zion went to Yedlnia."

That confrontation with my father in heder had a sobering effect on me. It was the last time I played hooky, but I was still far from accepting heder. I attended reluctantly and relished every free moment. In retrospect I realize that my errant behavior in heder was a reaction to my father's failure to give me the attention I craved. He was a charming and cultivated person, admired and respected as a leader. He was attentive to people in need, but he failed to recognize my need for his attention. He both loved me and neglected me. I remember when I was about nine my father took me along on a visit to the rebbe of Suchedniov. That was the one time I had him all to myself. He was attentive and loving. I also remember the first time he asked my opinion. I was then about thirteen. I even remember the house we were passing at that moment. It isn't surprising that I took out my frustration on the heder, the institution in which he had deposited me at the age of six.

I realize that my experience of heder does not characterize the institution that educated religious children in Poland. Its record is mixed, and our literature testifies to many instances of heder being remembered as a happy experience. Clearly, the personality of the melamed determined the atmosphere in his heder. Children attending the Horev and Yesodei Hatorah heders that were sponsored by the Orthodox party Agudath Israel were taught by trained teachers who inspired in their students a sense of community and cooperation. Regrettably, there was no Horev heder in Radom.

During the five years that I reluctantly spent in heder, I learned to read Hebrew fluently and to translate part of the Siddur, a major portion of the Humash with the commentary of Rashi, parts of the Prophets, the Book of Proverbs, the five Scrolls, and a little Talmud. I learned despite my inept teachers, because these subjects were necessary for me as a member of my family, where prayer and learning were a normal part of our daily life. I also learned to speak Polish correctly.

When I was twelve I went to the Torath Hayim yeshiva in Radom. It was named after the famous Rabbi Chaim Soloweitchik of Brisk, the rosh yeshiva (principal) in Volozhyn, the crown of yeshivas in eastern Europe during the nineteenth century where most of the leading rabbis and rashei yeshivoth (leaders of yeshivas) were trained. The lower grades of this yeshiva were located in a couple of rooms separate from the higher grades. This division was unfortunate because we missed the sense of being part of a yeshiva and the contact with older students who might have served as examples for us.

The teacher of my class, though knowledgeable in Talmud, epitomized the worst of heder teachers with none of the dignity one expected of a yeshiva teacher even in its lower grades. I don't remember his name, but I recall vividly his face, his attire, his temperament, and his manners. He was appallingly unsuited for being a teacher of young men at so impressionable an age. His face—the part of it not covered by his unkempt beard—was pockmarked and his eyes behind his glasses had a wild glitter about them, particularly when he was distraught, and that was the case most of the time. He tended to speak in a hurry, swallowing some of the words. He was impatient with our mistakes but absentmindedly forbearing. The only time he resorted to punishment, and that was a mild one, using his *gartel* (a cloth sash warn by Hasidim) was when the provocation led to the disruption of the whole class. Common inattention and restlessness of individual students he would attempt to correct with words, imploring or harsh. His salary must have been very low, for once on a Thursday his wife appeared in the class and made something of a scene, complaining that she didn't have enough money to prepare for Shabbat.

Every once in a while he would absent himself for several hours to attend to some problem at home, leaving us to rehearse our studies until his return. Most of us looked on these occasions as a respite from drudgery. Though we had graduated from heder and were devoting our time to the study of Talmud, our teacher was not able to lead us into the intricacy of the cases under discussion. His limited explanation of the text denied us the excitement it potentially held for us. Once again, as in heder, the study of Talmud was frustrating. When he left us alone we would spend our time in either conversation or some other diversion.

On one such occasion I had done something that finally broke the teacher's restraint in dealing with me. The teacher was called away on some emergency. We were playing peacefully when all of a sudden I noticed the soot in the back of the oven. I saturated my palms with the black soot and went over to the smallest student. In mock tenderness, I patted his cheeks with my sooted palms, telling him, "Yosele, you are such a nice boy." The boys burst out laughing. Just then the teacher returned and caught me in the act. My cruelty upset him deeply. He didn't punish me, though. Instead he said to me, "You will eventually become an apostate."

6

My Sisters' Education

The inferior status of women was not merely an inherited folk prejudice but a tradition rooted in the Talmud and the Codes, the sacred sources of Judaism. Women were not required to perform most of the positive commandments, including the commandment to study Torah. In the traditional home these laws led to a separation between boys and girls early in their lives. Boys stopped playing with girls around the age of five or six when they were sent off to heder. Girls were usually taught to read the Siddur and to read and write Yiddish. On Shabbat and holiday mornings a boy would accompany his father to prayers, but girls stayed home. These different roles produced pride and envy on both sides.

During the 1920s and early 1930s there were religious and secular schools for girls. Rayzel and Beila went to a Shabasuvka, a Polish public school that didn't meet on Shabbat. They studied Jewish subjects at Beis-Ya'akov, a religious school for girls that met in the afternoons and on Sundays. Their teacher, trained at the Beis-Ya'akov Teachers Seminary in Kraków, was a bright, articulate, and elegantly dressed woman, the product of Jewish culture in Galicia, where religious woman were under the influence of Viennese culture.

At Beis-Ya'akov, relations between teacher and students were cordial and the spirit of the school was cooperative. My sisters spoke affectionately about their teacher and were proud of their school. Their curriculum included the Siddur, Bible, Legends of the Talmud, Jewish law, and theological works of Rabbi Samson Raphael Hirsch and Rabbi Breuer. The language of instruction was Yiddish. In addition to formal education they also engaged in extracurricular activities, especially drama. I remember two plays that they staged around Hanukkah time. One of them was the *Sale of Joseph*, based on the story of Joseph and his brothers, and the other was *The Cantonists*, a play that dramatized the tragedy of Jewish child recruits under Czar Nicolas I—their resistance to conversion and their martyrdom. Girls played all of the roles. I was then about eight or nine; this was my first experience of theater, and I was sure that their acting was superb.

As students at Beis-Ya'akov, my sisters subscribed to the *Beis-Ya'akov Journal*, a well-edited monthly that I also enjoyed reading. My sisters' education was clearly richer and more enjoyable than mine. Compared to their school, heder was a disaster.

The Beis-Ya'akov school experienced phenomenal growth. Between 1917 and 1937 it grew from 1 to 250 schools with thirty-eight thousand students. It became a religious movement of young women that liberated its members from the inferior status that tradition had assigned to them, turning the gender difference from inferiority to distinctiveness.

The combination of public school and Beis-Ya'akov education had a liberating effect on my sisters, leading to economic and social independence. Their secular education opened up employment opportunities for them; Beila got a job in a bank, and Rayzel worked in our father's office. Their social independence also found expression in choosing a marriage partner. When the time came for Rayzel to get married, she rejected a match with a devout, erudite yeshiva student and chose instead Rachmiel, a worldly but religious businessman. After I had become a serious yeshiva student, my sisters found my piety exaggerated. I was fourteen at that time and my sex life consisted of wet dreams, after which I went to the mikvah to restore my purity. My sisters, not knowing the reason for my frequent visits to the mikvah, thought them to be acts of excessive piety and called me the "Mikvah Yidl."

Compared with my sisters, my education had no practical application. I studied to fulfill the commandment of studying Torah, for which I would be rewarded in the hereafter. In this world, Talmudic education had limited practical value. One could become a rabbi, a shochet, or a teacher of Talmud. Quietly, we were hoping for a good marriage with a *naden* (dowry) and several years of Kest (living with in-laws while studying and having children). When the period of Kest ended, a young scholar would use the dowry to start a business. In most cases these ventures failed, ending with the loss of the dowry. Thus the traditional education of boys led to an extended period of economic dependence followed by an uncertain future. I once asked my mother to loan me a quarter. Playfully she asked me, "Where will you get the money to repay me?" I answered, "When I grow up and get married I will receive a dowry and will repay the loan." That is how a traditional boy thought about his future. My sisters' education led to economic independence; mine led to extended dependence.

My sisters' education also discredited the notion that secular education inevitably led to alienation from tradition. My sisters, along with thousands of other Beis-Ya'akov students, remained devout. Though they knew Polish well and enjoyed reading world literature in Polish translation, they continued to speak Yiddish as a matter of principle.

I witnessed in my home two acceptable ways of being a religious Jew: mine, with an education that was limited to traditional Jewish texts and a smidgen of secular education; and my sisters', which led to enlightened Orthodoxy, proud self-awareness, and economic and social independence. Before I became a serious yeshiva student at the age of fourteen, I was proud of my sisters, envious of their new status, and confused by it. Afterward, our paths diverged and I became absorbed in my world of study and devotions. I believe that their enlightened Orthodoxy had very important implications for the future of Polish Jews. Alas, its further development was cut off by the tragedy that put an end to Jewish life in Poland.

7

Yeshiva

My Bar Mitzvah

Unlike most people, I have only a vague recollection of my Bar Mitzvah. I don't even remember preparing myself for it. At that time I was already studying Talmud in a junior yeshiva, I knew the Torah cantillations, and I certainly knew how to chant the Shabbat prayers, but I don't remember doing any of these as part of my Bar Mitzvah. The Shabbat of my Bar Mitzvah occurred in midsummer of 1936, when we were on vacation in Yedlnia, I remember being called to the Torah. After the service my family served the sparse summer community of mostly strangers a lean kiddush of sponge cake and vodka. Not even my father's sister, her husband, and their children, who lived only a few kilometers away, were there.

This was the first Bar Mitzvah in our family, and though Bar Mitzvahs were not celebrated lavishly in Poland, mine was definitely on the lean side. After so many years, it's difficult to recover the reasons for this unusual event. It may have been the result of my father's tendency to simplicity combined with our family's impoverished condition during the depression.

From Rebel to Devout Yeshiva Student

After heder some of my classmates went to work, others to learn a trade. Those who came from secularized well-to-do homes went to gymnasium. In Poland, secular education generally meant a break with tradition. Only a few went to a yeshiva. My family's being middle class and religious precluded my learning a trade. I assumed that my father wanted me to become a talmid chacham, a Talmudist. I thought that, like my father, I would study Talmud until marriage, then I would receive a dowry, get married, and spend a few years on Kest studying, and eventually go into some business. The question was where I should study.

While I was thinking about what to do with myself, Zvi Kaner, my friend with whom I had played hooky from heder, returned home for the holidays from the mekhina, a preparatory school of the famous Lublin yeshiva. He had spent a year there and came back a changed person. He was only fifteen, one year older than I. In heder both of us were irrepressibly boisterous, but now his whole manner had changed; he seemed to have become sedate, almost dignified, just what I imagined a young Talmudist should be. I was also impressed that older and more established scholars treated him as one of them. I liked what I saw. After questioning him about the mekhina, I made up my mind to go there.

To my surprise, my father, whom I expected to leap at the idea—for this was the first sign of my becoming serious—rejected it outright by saying, "Ben-Zion, if you want to study you can do so right here. I studied in Beit HaMidrash and I am no Am HaAretz [ignoramus]." My father had no use for famous brands, even when it came to yeshivas. More to the point, that yeshiva was attended mostly by Hasidic students, and he didn't want me to become one of them. He was critical of their mannerisms, their neglected appearance, their long *peyes* (side curls), their exaggerated piety, and their wallowing in tales of miracles supposedly performed by Hasidic rebbes. He was afraid lest I become like them.

This was in 1937, just after the Great Depression. At that time my father had already concluded that the future of Jews in Poland was bleak, and he was thinking about settling in Palestine. But I needed to make a decision before these plans crystallized. Had he told me what he had in mind for me, most likely he would have persuaded me; but he didn't, and I was already beyond being brushed off by a mere criticism or by his questioning the seriousness of my intentions. That only fueled my determination to act on my decision.

My father never talked to me about my future. Was it negligence? I rather think that he was reluctant to speak because he had become convinced that the old way of studying Talmud and cultivating one's piety was leading religious youth into a blind alley. He might have preferred that I join a religious Hakhsharah in preparation for settling in Palestine. Then why didn't he say so? He might have been afraid that change could lead me to break with tradition. It certainly was the case with most young people who went to work after heder.

When I consider whom my father chose to marry to Rayzel, I realize that it was he who had changed. Rachmiel was a young businessman. He was traditional but wore Western clothes. He was intelligent and amiable, but not learned.

I recall an exchange between my father and I on the subject of change that took place early in 1940. He had invited Professor Hurwitz of the local gymnasium for dinner. I arrived a few minutes late. My father introduced me to her, and instead of shaking hands with her, which was the proper way, I merely inclined my head toward her. After I took my place at the table, my father gave me a disapproving look. I remember thinking,

"He will tell me later what displeased him about my behavior." After dinner he said to me, "You should have shaken hands with Professor Hurwitz even if that meant that you would have to go to the mikvah." I didn't like his attitude and responded, "When you were my age did you shake hands with women? When you were my age did you bare your head in gentile company as you do now during the meetings of the city council? Consider what I might be doing at your age if I start with your behavior now." Instead of being angry, my father smiled at my reaction. He liked my getting the better of him in argument, just as he liked to have me beat him at chess.

Did my father expect me to find my way by analyzing his choices and preferences, as I have done in retrospect? In the absence of clear direction from him, I chose a way that was safe. Having been inculcated with the ideal of Judaism with dignity, I chose a yeshiva that embodied this ideal. It was an independent but also a safe choice for which he could not fault me. But I was aware that from his perspective I had chosen the wrong path, and this puzzled me. In retrospect I realize that he was right, that devoting all my time to Talmudic studies led to a cul-de-sac. But another choice required his guidance, which, regrettably, he did not offer. His argument that I could get my Talmudic education without going away was also disingenuous. He knew that times had changed. When he was young he swam with the stream, but I would have had to swim against it. The Beit HaMidrash and shtibl had ceased to be places where young men studied Talmud; to continue in the traditional path I needed the support of an attractive yeshiva.

Rachov

Nothing might have come of my decision were it not for the help I received from my mother. The yeshiva expected parents to pay for room and board, and I had no money of my own. In contrast with my father, my mother was consistently loving and supportive. Her hopes for me were not less than his, but her realistic view of life and her regard for the complexities of human motivation prevented her from spurning less-than-pure motives. There was also an element of self-assertion that played a role in her helping me. No one knew my father as well as my mother. She had a highly developed critical sense that she applied without favoritism to all persons and situations. Being a loving wife didn't prevent her from seeing her husband's blind spots. Thus, her love for me, her appreciation for my youthful fancy, and her critical stance toward my father led her to side with me and to provide the means I needed for going away to study. My mother had no funds of her own. It is remarkable that my father, despite being opposed to my decision, gave her the money for me to pursue an independent course. His doing so indicated his love and respect for her.

Shortly after the holidays in the fall of 1937, I took a train to Lublin on the way to Rachov, the small town in which the preparatory school was located. On the morning I left, my father went to his office as though nothing was happening. I was only thirteen and a half years old, this was my first trip away from home, and I would be gone for half a year, but all this seemed not to matter. He went to work without saying a word to me. And I, a chip off the old block, kept my peace. After he left, my mother took me to the train station, paid for the trip, and gave me pocket money. Apparently it was all worked out between them. The three of us performed our roles as if we had rehearsed them. I don't remember being troubled by my father's ignoring my departure.

My first act of independence and defiance was purchasing a pack of elegant cigarettes. I'd been smoking on the sly for some time, maybe a couple of years. My father must have known, for he had told me how he had quit smoking, but it didn't help. In my mind's eye I saw myself cutting quite a figure: I was wearing a new capote with a vest and was smoking cigarettes with a golden mouthpiece.

I stopped over in Lublin to spend Shabbat at Yeshivat Hakhmei Lublin, where I ultimately hoped to study. I was impressed by the imposing edifice, by its spacious halls, the beautiful Beit HaMidrash, the library, the clean dining hall, the tasty food, and the comfortable sleeping accommodations. I was equally impressed by the students. On Friday they were free to attend to their personal needs in preparation for Shabbat. Some were reviewing the Torah portion of the week and reading commentaries on the Bible. They were friendly but somewhat restrained, with a sense of personal dignity.

To an American these accommodations would be just what one would expect at a boarding school, but for its time and in Poland they were luxurious and extraordinary. Going to a yeshiva was associated not only with long hours of study but also with deprivation. In most yeshivas a student had to find his own accommodations. Students who came from poor homes would hire themselves out as night watchmen in a shop, which meant that they would arrive when the shop closed and they would be locked in for the night. As to food, the poor would be eating each day in a different home of householders who considered it a mitzvah to feed yeshiva students. The problem with this arrangement was that the student was subject to the mood of his host and the attitude of the maid who served the food. Some maids had become politically radicalized and viewed yeshiva students as freeloaders who did no "productive" work. Rabbi Meir Shapira, the founder of this yeshiva, felt that such conditions were not conducive to the development of self-respect. He aimed to match excellence of learning with attractive surroundings, to provide future rabbis with all their needs so that they would not lead the life of beggars.

My yeshiva was located in Rachov, an hour's ride by bus from Lublin. Before I left home I wrote to the administration, giving them the date and hour of my arrival, and asked that someone pick me up at the station. When I arrived, the *mashgiah* (dean of students) met me and took me to the yeshiva. Right then I had a feeling that I had overdone it: by asking that someone come to receive me I had behaved like a spoiled brat.

At the yeshiva I met Rabbi Isachar Leventhal, the rosh yeshiva, and Rabbi Shmaryahu Fensterbush, the town rabbi, who was its president. Both had studied with Rabbi Shapira in Lublin. Their dignified bearing and friendly but restrained welcome made a strong impression on me. Though relatively young, probably in their late twenties, they exuded an air of maturity and authority that reduced me to size, a brash youth of thirteen and a half. During the interview, which lasted about an hour, their eyes were focused on me and I felt as if they were reading my inner thoughts. When I was excused for supper I had the feeling that my interview hadn't gone well. After supper they called me back and told me gently that, being younger than most students, I could benefit from spending one more year at home. I recovered my composure and argued that if I were to return home people would assume that I had failed in some way, causing embarrassment to me and to my family. After a short consultation, I was finally admitted.

Rachov was a tiny hamlet with a spacious square surrounded by houses and stores. Several streets branched out from the square. The yeshiva was located half an hour's walk from the town. The study hall and dining room were located in a building large enough to accommodate about fifty people. We slept several to a room in nearby country houses.

The yeshiva wasn't far from the manor of the local landlord, which was surrounded by gardens and orchards. I of course assumed that the owner of the manor was a Polish nobleman. Several years ago I met the man whose family owned the manor and discovered that they were Jews.

The orchards were leased to Reb Shmariah, a simple, pious Jew. This was the first time I had met this type of Jew, ignorant but devout and close to nature. He treated the students in the yeshiva with affectionate respect and saw in us the saving remnant that would preserve the tradition. Reb Shmariah had a dog that he called Hitler. It was amusing to hear him say "Come, Hitler," and the dog wagged his tail and followed him.

In the middle of the summer Reb Shmariah would spend the nights in the orchard guarding the ripening fruit from being damaged by adventurous kids. On the night of Tishah b'Av, the fast commemorating the destruction of the Temple, he invited me to spend the night in his hut. The air was warm and fragrant, and while lying on a mat I could see the stars through the thatched roof.

At the mekhina there were about forty of us from all over Poland and Galicia between the ages of fourteen and seventeen, mostly sons of Hasidic families. The year was divided into two terms, with Passover and the High Holidays as our vacations. My adjustment to being away from home was by no means easy, and for a couple of months I longed painfully for home. I remember sitting in the field behind the yeshiva near a brook, my heart aching. I missed the tender and solicitous care of my mother as well as my sisters and brother. All the quibbling was forgotten, and my love for them turned into longing. I remember wondering what had possessed me to leave such a wonderful family. After a while, though, I became a member of my new community and the longing receded.

In December, several months after I had left home, my father came for a visit. I remember how pleased he was with the change he saw in me. He must have noticed that, whatever my initial motives might have been, I had become a serious student and a truly devout youth. His sparkling eyes illumined his handsome face with delight.

The transition from a boisterous boy to a serious young scholar was short, almost abrupt—an act of will. What made it possible was the supportive environment of the yeshiva, where all of us were going through a similar experience. From early childhood we were raised with the belief, which we recited in our daily prayers, that the Torah was a divine gift of love and that studying it was the greatest mitzvah. While conditions in heder and the first yeshiva made me contemptuous and unruly, the mekhina inspired respect that led to identification with the ethos of the yeshiva. The result was a life dedicated to the service of God in prayer and study with a fervor that only people in their teens are capable of. We spent all of our waking hours studying and praying, careful lest we waste a precious moment idling. That is where I first encountered the concept of *bitul zman* (nullification of time). In our society, killing time is not altogether negative, but in the yeshiva, time not used in study or prayer, with the exception of tending to basic needs, was considered wasted, nullified. For us, time was Torah.

We began and ended the day studying. In the morning we studied a tractate of the Talmud for *bekiuth* (to gain extensive knowledge). At nine in the morning, after prayers and breakfast, we assembled for a *shiur* (lecture) given by the rosh yeshiva that lasted two hours. That shiur focused on the text of a different tractate than the one we had studied on our own before breakfast. The shiur was by no means a solo performance. Students engaged the lecturer not only for clarification but also to argue for alternate interpretations. After the shiur we reviewed the text and reflected on the new insights presented by the lecturer.

We studied intensively until we absorbed the text with its interpretation. I remember one night a fellow who slept across the room from me suddenly sat up in his sleep and recited a page of Talmud. That day we had begun a new and difficult chapter. All of us had worked hard on it, and he apparently had committed it to memory. To this day, I still recall passages from what I learned then.

Equally intense were our devotions. I worked on focusing my thoughts during prayer and tried to avoid extraneous thoughts—not an easy task for a youth with an active mind. The most disturbing intrusions were sexual daydreams. I was chagrined that at the moment when I was addressing God I was troubled by my mortal needs. Often I immersed myself in the mikvah in preparation for the morning prayers, and once I almost drowned. I had gone at dawn, and no one was there. I didn't know how to swim, and proper ablution required immersion without contact with anything else. I had walked down the steps holding onto the rail. When I immersed myself I let go of it, and when I tried to come up I flailed about for a moment until I grabbed hold of the rail again.

Friday was devoted to preparation, including writing home. To make up for lost time on Friday, some students would stay up Thursday night to study. After lunch we went to the mikvah. During the afternoon we reviewed the parashah and read commentaries on it. Students who were already attached to a Hasidic rebbe would read his works and those of his predecessor. By sundown we were in our Shabbat garments ready to welcome the Shabbat Queen with a festive service.

The Shabbat meal was presided over by Rabbi Leventhal, and often also by Rabbi Fensterbush. Our tables were covered with white cloth, and the meal was served by waiters. The meal began with singing "Shalom Aleichem"—the hymn welcoming the Shabbat angels—and the chorus of forty young men resounded through the hall, enveloping all of us. Kiddush was chanted by Rabbi Leventhal or Rabbi Fensterbush. Between dishes we sang zmirot, the traditional Shabbat hymns. We conversed in hushed tones so as not to disturb the Shabbat tranquility.

Shabbat morning we rose an hour later than on weekdays. After the service and the noon meal we enjoyed leisure time. Most of us imitated our parents by taking a nap. One Saturday afternoon of a beautiful summer day several of us were lying on our beds, ostensibly taking a nap. Unable to sleep, we chatted about this and that. Suddenly, Zalman, a tall, blond fellow from Kuzmer (Yiddish for Kazimierz on the Vistula), interrupted: "You want to hear some marvelous and true stories?" All of us fell silent. Zalman then went on to tell us about a girl in his hometown who had died, and shortly afterward her parents were startled to find her at home doing laundry. Frightened and trembling, they went to seek the rabbi's advice. He told them that the girl might have been buried in soiled shrouds. On his recommendation her grave was opened and she was given clean shrouds, and after that she ceased to appear at home. There was silence in the room. After a while Zalman went on to tell us that in his town on Saturday evenings one could hear the groaning of a spirit under the bridge over the Vistula. Apparently the spirit was refusing to return to hell at the end of the Sabbath. For according to the Talmud the souls of sinners are given a furlough from hell over the Sabbath. I remember lying there brimming with excitement and thinking what a sheltered life I had lived, never having met a demon or a spirit. Of course, I never doubted their existence.

Hagigath Hatorah

Several weeks after Shavuoth we all went by bus to Lublin to participate in the Hagigath Hatorah—the Torah celebration occasioned by the completion of the Talmud. Rabbi Shapira had instituted the Daf Yomi, studying a folio page of Talmud each day to complete the Talmud in seven years. Thousands of people studied the Daf Yomi, and in the summer of 1938 the cycle was completed for the second time. A large number of people assembled at the yeshiva for the celebration, among them distinguished rabbis and Hasidic leaders.

At that time I was fascinated by Hasidic leaders and tried to meet as many as I could. Hasidism has an institution called Sholem Nemen, which consists of greeting the rebbe, and I wasted no time going from one worthy to another. I remember going to greet the Sadigerer rebbe, whose followers counted in the thousands. When I entered the room he was sitting with the Radziner rebbe, who, out of humility, refused to be honored along with the Sadigerer rebbe, who was his senior.

That morning as I was walking toward the yeshiva synagogue I saw, from the opposite direction, the Boyaner rebbe, a tall, handsome man in a beautiful tallith with a sparkling silver collar over his head that looked like a crown. He was surrounded by several students as if by an honor guard. He looked every bit like a prince, an image cultivated by the descendants of the Rizhin dynasty that introduced the concept of royal Hasidism. Overcome by what I saw, I stepped back reverentially. Years later I came across an eyewitness report that Reb Moishenew, as he was endearingly called, when facing death in Auschwitz, approached the ss officer in charge, grabbed him by his lapels, and shouted at the top his voice, "You despicable murderers! Think not that you will destroy the Jewish people . . . the Jewish people will exist forever, but you, despicable murderers, will cease to be a power. The day of reckoning is near. You will have to account for the blood you shed. Our blood will not rest until a fiery destructive fury will destroy your beastly blood." He spoke with great energy. He then put his hat on and shouted with mighty ecstasy, "Shema Israel" ("Hear O Israel"), the exclamation of Jews who were dying to sanctify the name of God.

Only two lectures were given during the celebration: one by Rabbi Menahem Zemba, a member of the Warsaw rabbinate and a distinguished Talmudist, and the other by a student, who gave the *Hadran*, meaning "we shall return to you." In a Hadran, which is usually given at the completion of a tractate, the speaker discusses major points of the tractate. In this instance it was a Hadran discourse at the conclusion of the whole Talmud. That student, whose name I no longer remember, displayed astounding erudition by ingeniously linking each of the tractates in the Talmud. In the evening students had returned to their studies, each of them chanting the text aloud. I remember standing next to my rosh yeshiva, who was listening to the cacophony emerging from the open windows; he turned to me and with satisfaction said, "Listen to the sound of Torah."

As we approached the end of the first term, my longing for home returned. The night before our departure, my excitement mounted to the point that I couldn't go to sleep and stayed up the whole night. But after a few days at home, the excitement waned. I began to miss yeshiva life, where I was a member of a community of peers. I had changed: at the age of fourteen I had become independent of my family.

Some of the things I had acquired in the yeshiva were a bit extreme and didn't sit well with my family, who themselves were devoutly religious but without the extra fervor I was experiencing at that time. When I returned from the mekhina, my sister Beila waited for me at the station. We were both excited to see each other. She hailed a *doroshka* (a horse-drawn cab), and the following conversation ensued: "I can't go with you." "Why not?" "I can't ride with a woman in a doroshka." "But I'm your sister." "Am I going to announce this to everybody?" In the end we rode together.

David Potashnik

During Passover vacation of 1938 I met a former classmate from heder, David Potashnik, who had gone to the gymnasium. After several meetings I succeeded in persuading him to drop secular education and come with me to the yeshiva. The rosh yeshiva gave him permission to attend only after I guaranteed that I would personally tutor my friend and bring him up to par with the rest of us. I kept my word. I remember studying with him twelve hours a day to prepare him for an exam. David became a devout Jew and a scholar. His father, Yankel Potashnik, a food and liquor merchant, was himself a religious Jew, but like many parents during the 1930s, he looked upon his children's secular education as an economic necessity, though he knew that it meant a break with the traditional way of life. David's interest was rekindled by my enthusiasm, and both of us were nurtured and sustained by the yeshiva.

Shavuoth at the Yeshiva

In the summer of 1938 I spent Shavuoth at the yeshiva. Shavuoth, the holiday that commemorates Kabbalath Hatorah, receiving the Torah, had special meaning for yeshiva students. We celebrated it as our Simhath Torah. That Shavuoth was enhanced for us by the presence of a distinguished guest from the Lublin yeshiva.

Rabbi Arye Leib Landoy, rosh yeshiva in Lublin, came to spend the holiday with us. Among Talmudists he was known as the Gaon (brilliant Talmudist) of Kolbiel, a small town thirty miles southeast of Warsaw. In addition to his learning, students admired Rabbi Landoy for his friendliness toward them. When I first visited the yeshiva of Lublin I met Rabbi Landoy. I was walking down the long hallway when suddenly I felt an arm on my shoulder; it was Rabbi Landoy. I came away from our brief encounter encouraged by his warmth and simplicity.

We began the holiday studying Talmud until shortly before midnight. After the evening prayer and the festive holiday meal we danced around the tables singing verses from Psalms. Rabbi Landoy danced with us. We danced vigorously for a long time; it tired even me, but Rabbi Landoy continued to dance with us.

That summer, shortly after Shavuoth, Pinye, my younger brother, died. When I returned home at the end of the term my parents were still suffering from the tragedy and asked me to stay home for the following term. After spending half a year at home and studying independently in the Kozhenitzer shtibl, I decided in the spring of 1939 to go away and study at a mekhina that had opened in Otwock under the leadership of Rabbi Avraham Mordeche Hershberg, whom I knew from Rachov, where he had been a tutor. Otwock, a resort near Warsaw, was famous for its woods, which perfumed the air in the summer with the fragrance of its pine trees.

Shortly after Shavuoth my father came to take me home. He stayed at the famous Gorevich pension that was frequented by the cream of Polish Orthodoxy. Shabbat morning after services

I joined my father for brunch. This was my first visit to a fancy pension. We sat at a long table, I opposite my father. On my right sat a wealthy Hasid of Ger. Among the guests were Pinie Levin, the vice president of the Agudah, and the son of Rabbi Elhanan Waserman, the famous principal of the Baranovitch yeshiva. I was in high company. The food was excellent, the variety and quality impressive: all sorts of smoked fish, cheeses, and the finest fruits of the season.

I no longer remember the drift of the conversation, but in the midst of it the Gerer Hasid on my right said, "Bialik, may his name blotted out." Suddenly my father's face turned red, and with obvious restraint he said, "Reb Yid! You should have washed your mouth before taking Bialik into it!" I was startled by my father's uncharacteristic sharp reaction. Among Hasidic Jews, Bialik was considered an *apikores*, a heretic. Bialik, who at that time was the foremost Hebrew poet, had once been a student in the famous Volozyn yeshiva, but he later ceased to observe traditional rituals of Judaism. I remember thinking, So, is that how far my father had come?

8

Jews and Poles

My political awareness began with the death of Marshal Joseph Pilsudski in 1935. I was then twelve, in my last year in heder. All of the students were taken to a movie theater to see his funeral train making its way from Warsaw, where he died, to Kraków, where he was to be buried in the Wawel, the burial place of Polish kings. Traditional Jews tended to view Pilsudski as a leader who was friendly to Jews. I don't know whether he was friendly or not, but I do know that the generals who ruled Poland after him were openly anti-Semitic. It is during that time, from 1936 until 1939, that I became an avid reader of *Dos Yidishe Togblat*, the Orthodox daily that our family subscribed to. An important and frightening part of the news was the anti-Jewish policy of the Polish government. We had no illusion about the anti-Jewish feelings of Poles, but government-sponsored persecution was ominous. It closed the doors of reprieve.

At that time there were more than three million Jews in Poland, numerous yet vulnerable. Jews were tax-paying and law-abiding citizens, but they were not Poles. Only Christians were Poles. Was this confusing? Not for the traditional child, for whom being a Jew or a Pole meant different religions, different holidays, different languages, different cultures, and different nationalities. Even our garments were different: religious Jews wore long black capotes and black flat hats with a short visor, whereas Poles dressed in European style. As religious Jews, we conceded that Poland belonged to "them" and that we were in exile, waiting for God to redeem us. We were a nation "sojourning," living in Poland only temporarily. But being "strangers" in a country where our ancestors had lived for centuries produced complex feelings about ourselves and about Poles.

Relations between Poles and religious Jews were burdened by prejudices on both sides. Just as our self-image was shaped by our religious tradition, so was our view of Poles. We were the descendants of Jacob, who, according to tradition, studied Torah and lived by its commandments. Poles, on the other hand, were the descendants of Esau, with all of the vile characteristics that our tradition ascribed to him: a depraved being, a murderer, a rapist, and an inveterate enemy of Jacob. This image of Esau, which developed two thousand years ago in reaction to the oppressive domination of the Romans, was transferred onto Christians who persecuted Jews. However, in our day-to-day contact with Poles these prejudices lay dormant until they were activated by anti-Semitic behavior.

Poles got their prejudices against Jews from the Roman Catholic Church. In 1936 Cardinal Hlond, primate of Poland, issued a pastoral letter to be read in all Roman Catholic churches of Poland. In it he declared: "A Jewish problem exists, and there will be one so long as the Jews remain Jews. It is an actual fact that the Jews fight against the Catholic Church, they are free-thinkers, and constitute the vanguard of atheism, bolshevism and revolution. The Jewish influence upon morals is fatal; their publishers spread pornographic literature. It is also true that the Jews are committing frauds, practicing usury and dealing in white slavery.

It is true that in the schools, the Jewish youth is having an evil influence, from an ethical and religious point of view, upon the Catholic youth. . . . Not all the Jews are, however, like that."

Then the cardinal urged an economic boycott of the Jews: "One does well to prefer his own kind in commercial dealings and to avoid Jewish stores and Jewish stalls in the markets, but it is not permissible to demolish Jewish businesses. One should protect oneself against the evil influence of Jewish morals, and particularly boycott the Jewish press and the Jewish demoralizing publications, but it is inadmissible to assault, hit or injure the Jews." Poland was then a deeply devout Catholic country, and the cardinal's letter was taken as official Christian truth. This poisonous pastoral was not exceptional; it was in keeping with other church publications that inflamed attitudes of religious Poles against Jews.

That same year, the economic boycott of Jews also received the approval of Poland's prime minister, Slawoj Skladkowsky. Speaking in the Polish Diet in June 1936, he declared: "Economic boycott, of course, but without violence."

These vicious attacks on three million law-abiding Polish citizens by the leaders of the Polish church and state came at a time when the Nazi regime had already stripped the Jews of all civil rights in Germany, and when England, under Arab pressure, had all but closed the gates of Palestine to Jews. One can imagine the sense of helplessness and desperation of Polish Jews.

The combined effect of religious prejudice and triumphant nationalism led to the official anti-Jewish stance of the Polish government. The nation's widespread poverty was attributed to Jews, whose livelihood was viewed as having been achieved at the expense of Poles. Consequently, Jews were subjected to economic discrimination. For example, in Radom, my hometown,

Jews were a third of the population, but only Poles were eligible for the numerous government jobs.

The harsh views of the cardinal and the prime minister were not lost on the National Democrats, known as the Endeks, a semi-fascist party that organized the boycott against Jewish businesses. I vividly remember seeing young men standing in front of Jewish stores with placards that said, "Nie kupoj u Zyda" ("Don't buy from Jews"). Despite having lived in Poland for centuries Jews were viewed as strangers. Graffiti appeared on walls and fences with the call, "Zydy do Palestyny" ("Jews go to Palestine").

Official anti-Semitism also led to periodic outbursts of violence and abuse. Once when I was a child I was standing on the sidewalk watching a military parade marching with a band. Like every child, I thrilled to the music and the rhythmic march of the neatly groomed soldiers. Suddenly a Polish boy hit me, shouting, "Zydzie! Kike! That's not your army," and spoiled the illusion. But a boy must have soldiers and heroes, and I had plenty of them. They all came from Jewish history, mainly from the Bible, but they didn't march. This was a comparatively mild but memorable experience.

During the 1930s, Jewish students at Polish universities were attacked by Polish students and forced to sit in separate sections. Those who chose to stand during the lectures rather then sit in these "ghetto" seats were attacked by their Polish classmates.

Official anti-Jewishness eventually resulted in pogroms in several towns. I was especially aware of the pogrom that took place in March 1936 in Przytyk, a small town near Radom, in which three people were killed, one of them a Pole, and twenty were injured. Houses were destroyed and stores plundered. Thousands of Jews in Radom marched in protest of the subsequent trial, which treated the Jews who had defended themselves as criminals.

Because Jews were a vulnerable minority, their prejudices never led to organized violence against Poles. Traditional Jews responded with contempt for both the people and their religion. We viewed Catholicism as idolatry. Poles were stereotyped as lechers and drunkards, given to brawling and wife-beating. I remember a popular Yiddish folk song about Jacob, the Jew, who rises in the morning and goes to the Beit HaMidrash to study and pray, and Esau, a Pole, who goes to the tavern. The refrain exclaims, "Oy! Shiker is a goy, a goy is drunk! And he must drink because he is a goy." Few religious Jews had any contact with educated and sensitive Poles, and when they met one he was seen as an exception.

Secularized Jews who didn't go to heder and secularized Poles who did not attend church were usually free of these prejudices. That explains the friendly relations among Jews, Communists, and Socialists. My father, an Orthodox Jew, had excellent relations with other city councilmen in Radom, most of whom were Socialists. In fact, our city was known as "Red Radom." Once, at a city council meeting, my father was in the middle of making a speech when an Endek came after him with a chair in his hand. He apparently didn't like what my father was saying. Fortunately, a Socialist councilman took the chair out of his hand and saved my father from harm.

But this is only one aspect of the story. Jews were well-organized politically and had elected representatives in every branch of government, in city councils, and in the national Diet and Senate. Some of the representatives were distinguished rabbis and communal leaders. I remember reading reports of verbal clashes between anti-Jewish representatives and Jewish senators or deputies. There were no Jews in the administration.

The official language of Poland was Polish. The language of religious Jews was Yiddish; it was what they spoke at home, and it was the language of their education in heder and yeshiva. In 1918, after Poland regained independence, the government decreed that Polish be taught in heder. That is where my generation learned to speak Polish. Most religious Jews who grew up before Poland became independent spoke Polish poorly with a Yiddish accent that was derogatorily called *Zydlaczic* (Jewing), a term used also by assimilated Jews. Some religious Jews spoke Polish correctly; my whole family spoke Polish well, especially my father. But religious Jews who knew Polish continued to speak Yiddish, not only because it was their native language but as a matter of principle. Speaking Polish was a sign of assimilation. Poles did not speak Yiddish unless they had grown up among Jews.

In my time most Polish Jews had broken with tradition. Some of them were Socialist Bundists, some Zionists, and some assimilationists. Bundists and Zionists spoke Polish and Yiddish and had publications in both languages. Assimilationists spoke only Polish, but Poles continued to view them as Jews despite their efforts to become part of Polish culture and society. Religious Jews looked on assimilationists with a mixture of pity and contempt. We felt that they had lost their self-respect as Jews and were still treated by Poles with contempt. We used to say, "Pol Zydem I pol Polakiem jest calym laidakiem" ("Half a Jew and half a Pole is a whole scoundrel"). Even those who took the final step and converted to Christianity were still viewed by Poles as Jews. I don't know how assimilated Jews coped with these degradations; they must have been more vulnerable than religious Jews, who were perfectly satisfied being Jews and didn't seek entry into Polish society.

However, it would be grossly unfair to give the impression that all Polish people wanted to harm Jews. I knew Poles who defended Jews, who did business and worked with them. Even in the worst of times, under the German occupation, some Poles—mostly Socialists or Communists—risked their lives to save Jews. Some Catholics, including priests and nuns, overcome by remorse or compassion, protected Jews who had managed to escape from concentration camps. It is remarkable that despite the vehement anti-Jewishness of the 1930s, Jews still fared better in Poland than they did in Germany, France, or Spain. Jews were never expelled from Poland.

Despite the traditional belief that we were in exile, our attachment to the natural environment of Poland was remarkable. After more than half a century, I still recall various parts of my hometown. In my dreams I sometimes walk its streets. I recall with pleasure my summers in the country, the endless woods where I collected berries and mushrooms, the orchards where I stole apples and plums, and our own garden with delicious cherries and sun-ripened tomatoes. Agnon, Israel's Nobel Laureate, describes affectionately the landscape and architecture of Buchach, his hometown. Bashevis Singer, also a Nobel Laureate, describes in his books a vast variety of Jewish and some Polish types over a period of four hundred years. Singer is equally attentive to the natural environment. His vivid descriptions of cities, small towns, and villages is memorable.

It occurs to me that Jewish submissiveness to Polish discrimination and persecution may have played a harmful role during the German occupation. Submissiveness is a survival tactic in which the vulnerable party controls its will when faced with a stronger opponent. Between 1918, when Poland regained its independence, and 1939, when it lost it, Jews reacted with restraint to repeated official and popular persecution and humiliation. This persistent submissiveness to Polish aggression may have weakened the Jews' will to survive when they were faced with the overwhelming power of the German occupation.

9

Rayzel's Engagement

When my oldest sister, Rayzel, became engaged in the winter of 1937–38, the other children of the family were surprised. She had never dated, nor had we seen a *shadchan* (matchmaker) visit our home. One day a young man came for dinner, after dinner he and Rayzel went for a walk, and the next thing we knew they were engaged. Clearly, my parents had conspired to bring this about, but how did it happen?

At twenty Rayzel was a stately brunette, feminine, gentle, and soft-spoken. After graduating from primary school she had attended Beis-Ya'akov, an afternoon school for religious girls, and was active in the Bnoth Agudath Israel, the girls' branch of Agudah, the Orthodox political movement in Poland between the two world wars. The school and the organization, though in the orbit of Orthodoxy, were progressive with a tinge of feminism. Many Hasidim considered their publication, the *Beis-Ya-akov Journal*, to be too worldly.

Rayzel had received many marriage proposals. A wealthy merchant had even offered a large dowry if she were to marry his son. I knew the young man: he had studied in the Lublin yeshiva and was admired by all his friends for his piety, erudition, and sensitivity, but he was too unworldly for Rayzel.

The year of Rayzel's engagement, my father did more traveling than usual. It was only later that we found out why. He had decided to meet every marriage candidate without revealing his true reason. When the shadchan proposed Rachmiel, my father went to Driltch (Ilza in Polish), a small town near Radom where Rachmiel's father owned lime pits as well as a leather store that Rachmiel managed. On arrival my father went directly to the leather shop, purchased some leather, and in the process struck up a conversation with Rachmiel that led to an invitation for lunch. Rachmiel had few out-of-town customers, and my father was a charming conversationalist. When they parted after lunch, he invited Rachmiel to visit him on his next shopping trip to Radom, the tanneries capital of central Poland. On returning home, he told the shadchan to bring Rachmiel to his office on his next visit to Radom.

The shadchan wasted no time. The following Thursday, the day Rachmiel usually came to do business in Radom, the shadchan contrived to meet him, took him for a walk, and when they passed my father's business, the shadchan invited Rachmiel to meet a friend of his, a very interesting man. At the office Rachmiel recognized my father and also met Rayzel, who worked there. After a brief conversation my father invited Rachmiel for dinner. At that point Rachmiel had probably caught on to what was happening. That evening after dinner he invited Rayzel for a walk, and that was the beginning of their romance. Several months later, in the spring of 1938, their engagement was announced and the wedding set for the late summer.

Rachmiel was in his mid-twenties, of medium height with an angular, calm face, alert eyes, and a disarming smile. He was friendly but somewhat restrained, and his glasses gave him the appearance of seriousness beyond his years. He dressed not in the traditional long Jewish garments, like my father and I, but in

European style. In Poland of the 1930s these were signs of modernity. He was also clean shaven, whereas my father had a full beard and I had the promise of one.

At that time I was studying at a Hasidic yeshiva and had become very pious, but I don't remember being bothered by the modernity of my future brother-in-law. Perhaps from the perspective of an uncompromising teenager I already saw my father, a businessman active in city affairs, as having made compromises. That is also how I viewed Rayzel: though observant, she had been "infected" by the secularity of her education and the literature she read. Choosing Rachmiel, a worldly though traditional young man, was only one more compromise for my father and was just right for Rayzel. I liked Rachmiel, and I was pleased that Rayzel was going to be married and that I would have a brother-in-law.

During 1936, the year before Rayzel became engaged, Polish Jews had experienced a wave of violent anti-Semitism. After the death of Marshal Pilsudzky, when the new prime minister encouraged a boycott of Jewish businesses and there had been a pogrom in Przytyk, Jews felt utterly vulnerable in the new Polish republic. My father, who was familiar with Polish politics, had come to the inevitable conclusion that Jews had no future in Poland. Though he was not formally a Zionist, yearning for Zion was part of his daily life. As a religious Jew he prayed many times in the course of the day for the return to Zion and Jerusalem. Hitler's rise to power and the stark political-economic conditions in Poland contributed to turning these messianic hopes into a practical plan for action. Only a return to Zion could save Jews from these dire circumstances.

This realization was also reinforced by my father's critical view of Jewish life in Poland. He was appalled by the neglect of practical education and planning for the future of the younger generation. At that time most religious Jews, especially Hasidim, gave their children only a religious education, leaving their economic future to God, and the results had been disastrous. How many heder teachers, rabbis, shochtim, and other minor religious functionaries could the increasingly impoverished community sustain? He was also troubled by the prejudice against craftsmanship or agriculture that was prevalent among religious Jews, and was dismayed by their preoccupation with tales of miracles attributed to Hasidic leaders and their disregard of the political and economic realities. Only a radical change such as the return to Zion could remedy these ills.

Rayzel's engagement was the occasion for us to take decisive steps. Rayzel, Rachmiel, and I would go to Palestine to set up a base for the whole family. My father's business had recovered from the economic depression of the early 1930s, and together with Rachmiel they had enough money to go to Palestine on a "capitalist" visa without having to wait for the British quota. Meanwhile, the engagement had enlarged our family, bringing cheer and new vitality Rachmiel's visits, festive dinners, and exchanges of gifts were happy occasions. In the spring of 1938, on my way home from the yeshiva, I visited Rachmiel and came away feeling that I had gained a relative.

10

Pinye's Death

Pinye was only two years younger than I, but when I was fourteen and he twelve it seemed like more. He was still in heder, and I had already gone through my rebellion against heder and confrontations with my father. At fourteen I was already a *yeshiva bocher*, a young man studying at the yeshiva of my choice.

There was also something else that set us apart. My parents had singled me out for special treatment because I was the first male child who survived birth. My parents showered me with affection. Even after I had grown up they were still telling sunny stories about my childhood. Pinye, on the other hand, received a full measure of their love without being singled out. He was a sweet-tempered child who behaved reasonably at home and in heder.

The spring of 1938 was a cheerful time in our home. Rayzel, my oldest sister, had become engaged, and Rachmiel, her fiancée, was coming to spend the first two days of Passover with us. A week before the holiday, Pinye complained of a stomachache and Dr. Goodman prescribed bed rest. When Rachmiel came, Pinye seemed to have improved. I still remember the smile on his wan face. But, several days later, as soon as Rachmiel had left, Pinye ran a high temperature and it became clear that he had more than a common stomachache. After examining him again, Dr. Goodman suddenly urged my parents to take him to Dr. Soloveitchik's clinic in Warsaw. There he was diagnosed as suffering from appendicitis. Before the discovery of antibiotics, that was a death sentence. For some reason, however, our parents did not share this information with us, and my sisters and I were led to believe that Pinye was getting better.

While our parents were away in Warsaw, Rayzel and Beila were busy managing my father's business and taking care of Esther, who was only eleven. Not aware of the seriousness of Pinye's condition and with nothing for me to do at home, I returned to the yeshiva.

Several weeks later I had a strange and stark dream in which Pinye told me, "I just died," and disappeared. I woke up startled by the dream. I wanted to call my parents, but it was five in the morning. The dream was so realistic that I was certain that it was true. When I called my parents later that morning, they denied that Pinye had died. I suppose they did this to spare me from having to observe *shivah* (seven days of mourning) at the yeshiva. According to Jewish law, after a month one observes only one hour of mourning.

I continued to inquire about Pinye's health, and that must have been very painful for my parents. One day, as I was studying, I was told that someone was looking for me. It was my mother. When I saw her I realized that something terrible had happened. My usually energetic mother was hesitant, her face drawn, her eyes sunken, a picture of bereavement. It's hard to imagine how much love it took to make that journey. As I sat in the low stool performing the ritual of mourning, my mind was filled with questions: Why had they denied his death? Why the secretiveness? Why was I prevented from mourning together with the family? Seeing my mother's pain, however, I asked no questions.

Neither I nor my sisters ever discussed Pinye's death with my parents. Their silence undoubtedly had much to do with a searing sense of guilt for having failed to act in time to save his life. I doubt whether we could have dispelled it, but speaking with us would have conveyed our abiding love and respect for them, something they badly needed at that time. The reverential distance between parents and their children, even grown-up children, was an unfortunate aspect of our culture.

A year later, in the summer of 1939, I was studying in Otwock, a resort town not far from Warsaw. Suspecting that a war was imminent, my father came to take me home. Before we left he took me to the small resort town where Pinye was buried. I stood at his grave numb, unable to grieve. Not having experienced his death, funeral, and shivah, I refused to identify Pinye with the pile of dirt before me.

I also think that events in my life during the preceding year had a lot to do with my inability to mourn him. The year before Pinye died I had began to think about what I was going to do with myself and decided to go away to study. I chose a famous yeshiva and managed to get myself admitted. I had hoped that my father would be proud of me; instead, he rejected my choice. I persisted, and with my mother's help, I got there. In retrospect I realize that I was looking for a way to establish my identity independent of my father. Being the son of a charming, erudite, and universally admired person wasn't easy, but being the focus of his critical surveillance could have been crushing if I hadn't gotten away. Wrestling with my father was for me as strenuous and fateful as Jacob's wrestling with the angel. I too came away limping but confirmed. During this uneven contest all of my energy was focused on myself, on fulfilling my goals. When I finally went away I left behind the whole family, including Pinye. It would have taken me years of maturing to become again a sensitive member of the family. Unfortunately, that was not to be. Within two years the German occupation radically changed our lives.

Pinye's death also had other tragic repercussions for our family. My parents had decided to settle in Palestine. My father had came to the conclusion that the future for Jews in Poland was bleak. The first step in the relocation of our family was to take place after Rayzel and Rachmiel got married. Following their marriage the two of them and I were to leave for Palestine. But the mourning for Pinye delayed their marriage for a year. They were not married until late in 1939, under the German occupation.

11

Finding a Tutor

In the fall of 1938, I returned from the yeshiva to spend the holidays at home. My parents were still in deep mourning for Pinye. I was now their only son, and my parents wanted me to stay home for a term.

I was fifteen and had studied in a yeshiva for a year. I already knew how to get through a page of Talmud on my own, but to plumb its depths I needed a tutor. The search for a suitable tutor began during Sukkoth. Soon the choice narrowed to two candidates: Itchel Morgenbesser and Rachmiel Gutman. I knew both of them from the shtibl of Piaseczno Hasidism where my father and I prayed on Shabbat and holidays and where each of them occupied a seat of honor on the right and left side of the Ark.

Rachmiel was a tall, stately man of about sixty with lively, penetrating eyes. His full salt-and-pepper beard made him look like a patriarch. He spoke in a mellow baritone that had a velvety quality to it, and his measured way of speaking commanded attention. Rachmiel had once been a wealthy merchant and was now retired. His wife had died and he lived alone, spending most of his time studying and teaching. He taught a daily class in Talmud to the Hevra Kadisha (Burial Society), of which he was a member. His only son, a physician, like most doctors, was not observant.

In his youth, Rachmiel had studied in a Lithuanian yeshiva where the emphasis was on a thorough and penetrating analysis of the text of the Talmud, a quality that he retained throughout his life. Even now, in his retirement, when he periodically served as a *borer* (arbitrator) in business cases, his arguments would be measured, clear, and succinct, as if he were presenting the merits of a hypothetical case in the Talmud.

Six months earlier, when I had come home for Passover, Rachmiel greeted me after the Shabbat services and invited me for kiddush. I was then barely fourteen and had studied in the yeshiva only half a year. Though Rachmiel often came to see my father, he had never spoken to me. Now I was a young scholar worthy of his attention, or perhaps my father, wanting to find out what I had learned, had arranged our meeting. Rachmiel's small apartment was tastefully furnished. The glassed-in mahogany cabinet displayed fine china and colorful crystal goblets. On the table, covered with a white tablecloth, were two goblets, a carafe of wine, and a plate with several slices of cake, indicating that the invitation had been planned.

After kiddush, we talked for a while about the yeshiva and what I had learned there. I was ill at ease and responded with terse answers, but his relaxed manner soon dispelled my shyness. After he had gotten a sense of where I was in my education, he proposed that we spend a while studying together. We read the first Mishnah of the tractate Kiddushin, which deals with the laws of marriage. Rachmiel explained these with a clarity that helped me to understand the brief laws presented in that Mishnah, and I came away from that session encouraged by his attention. Naturally, I was pleased when half a year later it looked as though he might become my tutor.

Itchel Morgenbesser, the other candidate, was in many ways the opposite of Rachmiel. From his seat of honor on the right side of the Ark, his presence was felt by his pregnant silence. I never heard him speak at the services, neither during nor after. He either prayed or studied, but we were always aware of his presence; he was to us an ideal of piety and learning. During the Torah reading he stood by the side of the reader, quietly correcting mistakes.

On Simhath Torah, the most cheerful of our holidays, Rachmiel taught us nigunim (melodies) he remembered from his student days in Lithuania. These melodies were full of longing, reminiscent of Byelorussian folk songs, and were different from the Hasidic nigunim of central Poland, which were influenced by Polish folk dances. When the celebration became boisterous, Itchel brought us back to dignity by rapping on his prayer book. I enjoyed the playfulness of the adults and resented Itchel's interference. I saw him as a gloomy old man who wouldn't permit anyone to have fun—a wet blanket. Of course I never said anything of the sort; Itchel was held in such high esteem that one dared not criticize him.

Itchel was in poor health, but it wasn't clear what ailed him. His face was flushed, and he walked slowly, which made him seem older than his mid-fifties. His wife, with the help of their two sons, ran a neighborhood grocery, and Itchel spent his time at home studying. His sons, in their twenties, were neither learned nor devout, but they preserved the outward appearance of piety. They wore the long coats and the round flat black hats with a short cloth visor traditionally worn by religious Jews, except that the coats were cut to fit and their caps were moved to the back of their heads, revealing a stylish haircut that was frowned on among Hasidim. On Shabbat they came to services late wearing starched white shirts and colorful ties. It was obvious that they made an appearance out of respect for their father.

My father had known Itchel for a long time. Their relationship went back to the time when my father was my age. My father had been studying in the city Beit HaMidrash, where he had gained a reputation for being able to explain complicated passages in the Talmud in clear and simple words. Eventually, so many of the younger students sought his help that it interfered with his own studies. At about that time a new shtibl was founded by the followers of the rebbe of Piaseczno. They had become numerous enough to afford their own place of worship. This new shtibl was furnished with a basic library of rabbinic works, the Talmud, its Commentaries and Codes—the indispensable reference works for a Talmudic scholar. It also had an assortment of Hasidic books, particularly those written by the rebbe of Piaseczno and his predecessors. The shtibl was not in much use during most of the week and was located near my father's home. One day, when the number of interruptions had reached the limit, my father gathered up his books and moved into the new shtibl. The only other person who regularly studied there was Itchel, a recently married young man on Kest.

The shtibl had purchased the Warsaw edition of the Talmud—probably because it was cheaper than the Vilna edition—but it was not edited as carefully. From time to time my father would come across mistakes, particularly in the Commentaries that were printed in small letters. After careful consideration, he would suggest a correction in the margin. One day when Itchel came across one of my father's corrections, he called him over and asked him, "Who gave you permission to make corrections?" As my father tried to explain his reasons, Itchel became impatient and told him that he was too young to have presumed.

No one had ever treated my father with such contempt, and, being certain of his grounds, he was determined to vindicate himself. At home, in his father's library, they had the Vilna edition of the Talmud. He rushed home, took out the volume, and, sure enough, the text read as he had corrected it. Instead of eating supper, he rushed back to the shtibl. Itchel was still there poring over his books. When my father showed him the reading in the Vilna edition, Itchel paled. He had insulted a young scholar, unjustly accusing him of ignorance and arrogance. Itchel was beside himself. Overcome by contrition, he begged my father to forgive him, and from then on he treated him with respect.

What my father admired in Itchel was not only his learning and piety but also his candor and integrity. Itchel may have lacked Rachmiel's social graces and charm, but he was an uncompromising man of truth, unsullied by worldliness. Rachmiel dressed impeccably, his walking cane had an engraved silver handle, and instead of the flat Jewish cap he wore a black fedora. His sartorial elegance along with his dignified appearance and impressive manner of speech earned him the nickname "the Cardinal." My father liked Rachmiel and enjoyed his company, but he thought him a bit theatrical and vain.

Itchel considered it an honor that my father had chosen him to instruct me, and he was determined to succeed in this sacred trust. We started on the first Sunday after the holidays. I went to his apartment twice a week for a two-hour session. The room in which we studied served as both a living room and a bedroom; it was furnished with two sturdy beds, a large dining table, and half a dozen chairs, all in a dark mahogany.

Itchel may have been pleased to have me as a student, but from the way he behaved I would never have known it. His shyness made him ill at ease, and he wasted no time on conversation. As soon as I arrived we began to study. At first his voice was strained, but when we got into the subject he loosened up and spoke fluently. His eyes would light up, and his angular face became animated.

We studied the tractate Beitzah, which deals with the laws of the proper observance of holidays. As a subject of practical importance, this was discussed in rabbinic literature for nearly two thousand years, first in the Talmud, then in the Commentaries, the Codes, and the Responsa literature. Each time the subject was reviewed, something new was added. Itchel was truly erudite: he knew what each source had to say. I was probably his first student, and out of affection for my father he was determined to share his erudition with me.

Itchel assumed that I understood the overall significance of the subject and could appreciate the particulars of the extended debate. Slowly, in his hollow, colorless voice, he presented one interpretation after another. For several days I followed him and was impressed by his erudition. Then the line of argument became tenuous, the distinctions blurred, until I lost the drift of his thoughts. I sat gaping at him as he built castles in the air and destroyed them to build new ones. My mind wandered, and I was overcome by sexual daydreams while sitting in front of an open Talmud folio. After a while, I found a face-saving excuse and went back to study on my own in the shtibl.

Choosing Itchel was a mistake. He was indeed a scholar and a man of integrity, but he was reclusive. I doubt whether my father ever had a conversation with him. I would have preferred to study with Rachmiel, but nobody had asked my opinion. I too felt that it would be a privilege to study with a saintly person, but saintliness comes in a variety of forms. In addition to Itchel's reclusiveness and lack of experience in teaching, there was no chemistry between us. Our personalities were so different: I was a lively youth, he a sickly, depressed old man. I respected his learning but had no desire to be in his company.

The fiasco with Itchel was demoralizing. In the first year of my yeshiva education I had studied diligently. Now the diligence was gone. I went daily to the shtibl and sat before a Talmud folio, but I felt like I was marking time. It was not until a year later, when I returned to the yeshiva in Otwock in the summer of 1939, that my diligence returned.

12

The Beit HaMidrash and the Yeshiva

The Beit HaMidrash was the center for prayer and study of the whole community. Before World War I, after finishing heder young men continued their studies in the local Beit HaMidrash. In cities with a larger Jewish population people studied also in Hasidic conventicles called shtibls. The Beit HaMidrash in Radom was a large, rectangular hall furnished with long tables and benches; its walls were lined with bookcases stocked with Bibles, Talmuds, Commentaries, Codes, Responsa, and Hasidic and ethical literature of all periods.

At the center of the Beit HaMidrash was a *bimah*, a raised platform where the Torah was read. Opposite the bimah, on the eastern wall, at an elevation of several steps, stood the Aron HaKodesh, the Holy Ark, containing the Torah scrolls. Below the Ark to the right was the *amudah*, the prayer leader's stand. On both sides of the Ark were the seats of honor occupied by the rabbi and the leadership of the community. Women were seated in a balcony and were invisible to the men.

The Beit HaMidrash was open from before dawn until midnight. Morning prayers began at dawn, and as soon as one *minyan* (quorum of ten males) finished, another began. By midmorning several services had taken place. People who spent the day working would come early—some recited Psalms, some studied a chapter of Mishnah, others a page of Talmud, then joined a minyan, recited the morning prayers, and went home for breakfast.

In winter afternoons, when beggars had finished their rounds they would congregate around the heated stoves, telling each other stories about the day's adventures. In the late afternoon people who worked for a living returned for *minhah* and *maarib* (afternoon and evening prayers). After minhah, while they waited for evening to come, most of them would study. That was also the time when a *maggid* (an itinerant preacher) would mount the bimah and deliver a sermon. Most of the maggidim seemed to be well informed about heaven, and particularly about hell. They would describe in a somber singsong the bloodcurdling punishments meted out to deceased sinners, and the people wept copiously. I suppose these were their horror movies.

In the course of the day, several groups occupied the Beit HaMidrash. There were the Zaydene yunge-layt (silken young men), the newly-wed promising young scholars on Kest. Then there were the *batlonim*, older men whose wives earned a livelihood to support the family while the men were studying Torah and piling up a hefty portion in the world to come for themselves and their wives. Then there were old men who no longer worked but sat and studied. Alongside these mature scholars, some of them masters in rabbinical literature, and under their supervision sat those who had recently finished heder.

It was a unique, voluntary system of higher education without formal appointments, salaries, budgets, or administration. The older scholars instructed the younger ones and kept an eye out for promising young Talmudists, whom they would bring to the attention of the rabbi. Though young, some of them only thirteen, having become independent scholars, they needed no further surveillance than that provided by the ethos of the Beit HaMidrash. Studying Torah was a great mitzvah, and being a young scholar in the Beit HaMidrash was a privilege few would abuse. In the evening one could find three generations of a family sitting side by side and studying in the Beit HaMidrash: the father, who came to study after a day's work; the grandfather, who was retired and spent the day studying; and the grandson, who continued his studies after finishing heder.

The Beit HaMidrash produced *lamdanim*, people who were thoroughly versed in traditional Jewish literature, particularly the Talmud, its Commentaries, and the Codes. Here the rabbis and lay leaders of Polish Jewry were educated, including some of its political leaders. This culture of ubiquitous learning also produced a language of its own—lomdish Yiddish, the "scholar's Yiddish." The very term *lamdan* (scholar), derived from the Hebrew root l-m-d, is a Yiddish creation that returned into modern Hebrew in its new meaning.

The religious culture of the Beit HaMidrash was dealt a crippling blow during World War I. Poland and Galicia became the battleground of Russians, Austrians, and Germans. Some Galician Jews fled to Vienna and Hungary. Polish Jews were evacuated by the Russians from all the frontline towns and villages. Some towns were completely destroyed by the battling armies. People lost their moorings, their social standing, their livelihood, and authority over their families. The success of the Russian Revolution made it seem as though the "messianic" promises of Socialism were about to be fulfilled. Indeed, for several years at least, Jews enjoyed unprecedented freedom in the Soviet Union. In addition, the Balfour Declaration gave Zionism a measure of legitimacy it didn't have before. Challenged by assimilationist Jews, who broke with tradition under the influence of Western culture, secular Zionism, Socialism, and Communism, the traditional way of life declined, and by the end of that war the study of Torah had fallen to an all-time low.

When I was growing up during the 1930s, the Beit HaMidrash was used mainly for morning and evening prayers, and only one out of the twenty shtibls in Radom was frequented by young Talmudists. The others were used for daily and Sabbath prayers and stood empty the rest of the time. Here and there one would encounter a young scholar on Kest spending the day studying in a shtibl. What had recently been the norm became in my time an exception. In cities with large Jewish populations, such as Warsaw and Lodz, one could still find shtibls full of young men studying, but on the whole the traditional community was on the defensive and losing ground. In an effort to save the remnant, yeshivas were organized creating supportive environments, with teachers and *mashgihim* (spiritual guides) to protect students from the corrosive influences of the political and ideological movements active in the Jewish community.

By the late 1930s there were already many yeshivas in Poland, including a network of Keter Torah yeshivas sponsored by the Hasidic leader Reb Shlomo of Radomsko, who was independently wealthy and used his fortune to support them. There were also several Tomchei Temimim yeshivas sponsored by the rebbe of Lubavitch. At that time also, the Musar yeshivas spread from Lithuania into Poland. These yeshivas, called Beis-Yosef after Rabbi Yosef Yoizl Hurwitz of Novogrudok (Nowogródek in Polish), who inspired them, emphasized the study and meditation of ethical and moral literature alongside the study of Talmud.

In a category all by itself was Yeshiva Hakhmei Lublin. Though founded in 1930, it enjoyed a reputation of excellence and distinction from its very beginning. Its founder, Rabbi Meir Shapira, one of the most gifted rabbinical leaders of interwar

Poland, was aware of the sociopolitical conditions in the Jewish community. In 1919, at the age of thirty-two, he was already chairman of the educational committee of Agudath Israel, the Orthodox political party founded in 1912 to counter the inroads of Socialism and Zionism into the ranks of Orthodoxy in Poland. A year later he became its president. In 1923 he was elected deputy to the Polish Sejm, from which he retired a year later to devote himself to his educational goals. Chief among them was the establishment of a national yeshiva that would develop in its students the dignity they needed to become the leaders of the next generation. In his words, it was "a yeshiva that would raise the glory of Torah."

Yeshiva students used to eat *teg*; that is, each day they ate in a different home and slept wherever they could, some on a bench in the women's section of the synagogue, some as night watchmen in stores where they would be locked in for the night. Rabbi Shapira, deploring this situation, declared: "I have a dream of a great yeshiva, more beautiful and larger than any before. In my time yeshiva students will no more spend their nights as watchmen in warehouses and eat like beggars every day in a different house. I'll build them a royal palace." And that is what he proceeded to do. When I visited the yeshiva in 1937, I was impressed by the beauty and spaciousness of its halls, the attractiveness of the living quarters, and the quality of the food—not at all what one had expected of a yeshiva. Lublin was more than a yeshiva: it was meant to be a model institution that would raise the image and dignity of yeshiva studies and serve as the symbol of a renewed orthodoxy.

The opening of the Lublin yeshiva in 1930 was a national event, and though I was a child of seven, I followed the press reports. Present at the opening, alongside the rabbinic and lay leadership of Polish Jewry, were representatives of the government and the press. No yeshiva had ever opened in such an impressive manner. During the decade of its existence, the yeshiva became the pride of traditional Jewry in Poland. Press coverage, particularly by *Dos Yidishe Togblat*, the organ of Agudath Israel, played an important role in spreading and enhancing its reputation, not only in Poland but also abroad.

The attractive building that once housed the yeshiva has survived the ravages of the Holocaust. It now is the home of the Medical Academy of Lublin. During a visit to Poland in the spring of 1984, Professor Chone Shmeruk of the Hebrew University in Jerusalem protested the absence of a marker designating the origin and former use of the building. As a result of his intervention, a celebration, attended by government officials, took place in June 1985, and a plaque was dedicated. It states, in Hebrew, Polish, and Yiddish, "In this building was Yeshivath Hakhmei Lublin in the years 1930–1939." Even after its demise, Lublin is the only yeshiva in eastern Europe that has an official marker.

13

Encounters with Hasidism

Reb Yosele

I first encountered Hasidim when I was seven or eight. We had moved into a large apartment building with a big courtyard, and our neighbor across the courtyard was Reb Yosele, a leader of Hasidim.

When I first met him, Reb Yosele was in his late sixties. He had large blue eyes, high cheekbones, and a prominent nose. His white beard elongated his face and enhanced its light coloration, making him look like the portrait of a saint. Reb Yosele was a mild, soft-spoken person, without pretensions or affectations. His days were spent in prayer, study, and ministering to people who sought his advice and blessings. I never saw him without a book.

Before becoming a rebbe, Reb Yosele served as the rabbi of Wonchotsk and later Wierzbnik, small towns in the vicinity of Radom. Hasidic leadership had become dynastic, and sons of Hasidic leaders would seek ordination and serve as communal rabbis until they inherited a following.

Though *rabbi* and *rebbe* are variants of the same Hebrew word, they denote two different functions. A rabbi is the religious leader of a community. To qualify for such post he must be ordained by at least one rabbi who examines him in Talmud and Jewish law. When a community invites a rabbi he is given a contract that specifies his duties and his salary. Among his duties are to supervise *kashruth* (Jewish dietary laws) and institutions of Jewish learning and to decide cases of personal and business conflicts according to Jewish law. As the religious leader of the community he works with its elected leaders to assure the welfare of its people.

A rebbe, on the other hand, is a leader of Hasidim. He is their spiritual mentor and intermediary between them and God. He requires no ordination, nor is he accountable to anyone. Being a descendant of a rebbe and having followers—Hasidim who seek his advice and blessings—make him a rebbe. The Hasidim also sustain the rebbe and his family economically.

Reb Yosele was a descendant of Reb Yaakov Yitzkhoq, the "Holy Jew of Pszysche," who lived at the beginning of the nineteenth century. Reb Yosele became a rebbe when his father, Reb Pinhas of Kinsk, died and some of his father's Hasidim chose to follow him rather than his brother. Having observed the rituals of Hasidic leadership in his father's home, Reb Yosele practiced them with winsome humility.

On Yom Kippur, a day when most Hasidim visit their rebbe, about 150 Hasidim would come. Over time the numerous Hasidim of the "Holy Jew" had been divided and subdivided among his descendants, and they had been reduced further by the secularization of Jewish life in the twentieth century. There were still large and famous Hasidic courts with thousands of Hasidim like Alexander, Belz, Ger, Lubavitch, and Sadiger. Alongside them were several hundred rebbes, each with a small number of devoted followers who derived spiritual and emotional support from their rebbe and in turn provided for his meager worldly needs. Reb Yosele was one of them.

At my age neither the number of Reb Yosele's Hasidim nor his fame mattered. In fact, the small number of his followers worked to my advantage, making it possible for me to get his attention. I liked the blend of reverence and conviviality that characterized his community, especially the joyous celebrations of Shabbat and holidays. His Hasidim, mostly people who worked hard to earn their livelihood, were uplifted and felt closer to God by his presence. Reb Yosele and rebbes like him kept the Hasidic way alive, giving inspiration and solace to Jews who were living in times that were difficult both economically and politically.

My father was a much-admired communal leader, and Reb Yosele treated him with considerable regard. My father was respectful but circumspect. His father had been a Hasid of Reb Yosele's brother, and my father didn't want to give the impression that he was becoming one of Reb Yosele's followers. Occasionally the rebbe would invite my father to his Tish. On these occasions Reb Yosele would have him sit first on his right. I don't know how much my father enjoyed the honor, but it was a thrilling experience for me.

The Tish was an important Hasidic ritual observed on Sabbaths and holidays when the rebbe had a festive meal in the presence of his Hasidim. Hasidim believed that the *shirayim* (the leftovers from the rebbe's meal) were potently blessed. When the large plate with the remains of the rebbe's food was put in the middle of the table, Hasidim reached for the shirayim as if their life depended on it. The term for this activity was "khapen shirayim" ("grabbing shirayim"). Between courses they sang zmirot. That was followed by the rebbe's discourse, which Hasidim called *Toire*, a term generally reserved for Scripture. Before

Grace, a shammash named Motel would announce the names of Hasidim who stood wine for the Tish.

The rebbe's youngest son, Yedidya, Yedidya's wife, Shosha, and their two daughters, Rachel and Hasia, lived with the rebbe and were supported by him. Yedidya was an unfortunate by-product of Hasidic life. His education was limited to traditional Jewish texts, in which he did not excel. He had no business, and as the son of a Hasidic rebbe it was not proper for him to learn a trade. Though observant, there was nothing spiritual about him. I never saw him with a book; he spent most of his time reading newspapers and smoking. His wife was an attractive woman with no formal education. There was something feline about her. I remember her sitting in the window sunning herself. Their daughters, giggly and playful little girls, treated me like an older brother. I was still a boy and I enjoyed their attention. I was handy with gadgets and knew how to fix electric fuses. That's how I first came to the rebbe's attention.

After I had begun to study Talmud, the rebbe would invite me to study with him. On one such occasion, his wife had served him a cup of tea with several cubes of sugar. The rebbe, having become absorbed in the text, chewed up the sugar absentmindedly. When he was ready to drink the tea, he looked for the sugar, mumbling, "Well, well, she is becoming absentminded, she has forgotten to bring the sugar." When I told him that he had chewed it up, he smiled sheepishly. After one of these sessions, he told me that the word *Zion* has the same numerical value in Hebrew as the word *Yosef*, which was his name. In addition to being Ben-Zion, a son of Zion, I now was also Ben-Yosef. The rebbe was close to seventy and had only granddaughters. That is how I informally became his adopted grandson.

Once, on Kol Nidrei night, the Beit HaMidrash and all adjacent rooms were crowded with Hasidim in tallith and kittel, awaiting the rebbe's arrival. When the door of his study opened and the rebbe came out, all eyes were focused on him. He made his way slowly between them to his place near the Ark. When he passed me he stopped, looked at me affectionately, and said, "Bentzeeyen! Do you have a question that you would like to ask me?" I was startled but quickly recovered and asked him, "In one place in the Talmud it is written that a person should feel that 'the whole world was created for me,' and in another it says that a person should feel that 'I am but dust and ashes.' How is one to reconcile these conflicting teachings?" And he said: "One of these should be in your right pocket, the other in the left, and you should walk between them."

Yom Kippur, the climax of the religious year, was particularly intensive for Hasidim who were celebrating it with their rebbe. Reb Yosele's style was restrained and natural. On Yom Kippur, amidst his Hasidim, he reflected their love and reverence. In his presence they were attuned to every word he uttered and every sigh that accompanied it, and their prayers were more ardent. Reb Yosele used to recite the Shma slowly, enunciating each word as if he were counting gems. After we had finished the prayer we listened to his small but emphatic voice concluding the reading of Shma: "Lma'an tizkeru va'asitem at kol mitzvotai" ("That you may remember and perform all of My commandments and be holy unto your God"). These words, though spoken softly, found their way into our hearts. Many years have passed since that service, yet often when I recite the Shma I can hear his voice. To this day, echoes of it lift my prayers.

As soon as the Yom Kippur services ended, the mood of the Hasidim changed. Throughout the day they had pleaded, with tears in their eyes, for their lives. Now, at the end of a long day of fasting and prayer, they were confident that, with the rebbe's help, the heavenly scales were tipped to the side of mercy, their prayers were answered, their sins pardoned, and they were entering a new year with a clean slate. When that service was over, the Hasidim, assured of God's forgiveness, in a flare of energy, burst forth in song and dance, oblivious to their weariness and hunger. That was where I first saw adults singing and dancing. It was a welcome contrast to my father's solemn piety.

On the following day the Hasidim had a private meeting with the rebbe. That meeting was an important Hasidic ritual for which a Hasid prepared himself by having Motel shammash, the rebbe's personal attendant and secretary, draw up a *kvitel*, a detailed note requesting the rebbe's blessings on personal, domestic, and business needs. Upon entering the rebbe's chamber, the Hasid stood at the door until the rebbe invited him to approach and sit down. The Hasid then deposited on the table the kvitel with a *pidyon* (ransom, a sum of money for the redemption of the Hasid's soul). The rebbe examined the kvitel and gave his advice and blessings. Upon leaving, the Hasid retraced his steps while facing the rebbe, the way a devotee leaves a shrine.

One of the Hasidim who didn't leave was Reb Hayiml, a short, slender man of about sixty-five. He stayed through Sukkoth to serve as the rebbe's shammash, a privilege recognized by Motel, the rebbe's year-round shammash. I never heard Reb Hayiml say anything; I only remember seeing him whisper his prayers while facing the wall so as not to be distracted, or quietly serving the rebbe's meal, yet he remained indelibly in my memory. After sixty years I can still see him standing at the entrance of the sukkah reciting the Ushpizin—inviting, in Aramaic, the Patriarchs to the sukkah. I continue to wonder what significance I attached to him; I suppose Hayiml was ethereal enough to become identified in my mind with those spiritual guests.

On Yom Kippur of 1939 we prayed at Reb Yosele's. It was two weeks after the Germans had occupied Radom, and the mood was somber. We had no inkling of the tragedy that was to put an end to Jewish life in Poland, but we were all frightened, burdened with forebodings. Late in the afternoon, two plainclothesmen interrupted the service. They had come looking for Yonah Zilberberg, the president of the Jewish community of Radom. That was the last we saw of him. That interruption of the Yom Kippur service was for me a rip in time.

On Hoshana Rabbah of that year Reb Yosele led the Hoshana prayers. During the procession around the bimah, he stepped slowly, the lulav and ethrog in his hands like the symbols of royalty, and the silver collar of his tallith covering his head like a crown. At the end of each verse he halted, lifted his face, and exclaimed with a deep sigh, "Oi, yoi, yoi, Hoshana!—Please help!" I can still hear his pleading, plaintive voice.

One evening several weeks later, while we were still under curfew and blackout, I went across the courtyard to Reb Yosele's Beit HaMidrash, took out the tractate Sanhedrin of the Talmud, and studied the section that describes Hevlei Mashiah—the pangs of messianic times. I was convinced that the terrors of the German occupation were the suffering described in the Talmud that was to precede the coming of the Messiah. The small candle on the table cast the sizable hall in shadows.

Reb Ahrale of Kozhenitz

The Hasidic way at Reb Yosele's Beit HaMidrash introduced me to a way of life that I found attractive. My interest in Hasidism increased during the year I spent at a yeshiva whose students came from Hasidic homes in all parts of Poland and were themselves budding Hasidim.

When I was still a boy, Reb Ahrale had come to visit his Hasidim in Radom. He was the guest of Shmerl Korman, a wealthy leather manufacturer whose apartment was ample enough to provide living quarters for the rebbe and a large room that served as a synagogue. Reb Ahrale rakishly called his host "Shmerele ganev" ("Shmerele thief").

During that visit a woman had come to ask the rebbe's blessing. She was the sole breadwinner of her family and made a living selling oranges on the street. Oranges were expensive in Poland and were purchased as a special treat for someone sick or as a gift. She had sold her last basket and didn't have enough money to replenish her stock. Reb Ahrale told her to borrow a case of oranges and bring it to him. The woman did as bidden; toward evening she returned with a case of oranges and delivered them to the rebbe. At that time the house was full of Hasidim. The rebbe took the case of oranges, emptied it on the rug, and called out, "Eat, Jews, eat." The Hasidim needed no prompting, and in a few minutes not an orange was left on the rug. The woman stood on the side watching, her face pale, biting her lips. These oranges were all she possessed, and they were all gone. Then the rebbe shouted, "Shmerele ganev, lock the door," and to the Hasidim he said, "You have eaten oranges, now pay." In no time the woman had enough money to replenish her stock. This was a new type of Hasidic "miracle," and I liked it.

Reb Ahrale had many followers in my town, and they established a shtibl of Kozhenitzer Hasidism where they met for worship, study, and celebration. The shtibl was a source of information and gossip about the rebbe. The Kozhenitzer rebbe was one of the most controversial Hasidic leaders in Poland of the 1930s. He was revered by his Hasidim, reviled by the followers of his younger brother, who set himself up as a rival, and controversial because of his independent style. His behavior with Hasidim often was odd: at times it included insults and even an occasional slap in the face. But his Hasidim, in their devotion to him, interpreted his strange behavior favorably. The only Hasid

I knew was Shmulik Margulis, who came from a large and highly respected family. Shmulik was several years older than I, and he was a student at the famous yeshiva of Lublin. I felt that a rebbe who commanded Shmulik's devotion had to be a person of real depth.

Reb Ahrale used to spend his summers in Otwock, a resort not far from his home in Warsaw. In the summer of 1939 I studied at a yeshiva in Otwock. One Shabbat I went to observe the rebbe's Tish. During the summer it took place outdoors, in the woods near his villa. The first thing that was unusual was that two jesters sitting together performed at Reb Ahrale's Tish: they performed from their seats with rhythmic body movements and facial gestures, but the main show was the rebbe. He had a magnetic personality and was not constrained by the usual Hasidic ritual. He played his role with great charm and enjoyed it.

During that visit I was standing behind the rebbe next to a man who was wearing an elegant white summer suit and tie; he too had come to see the performance. Shirayim, food from the rebbe's plate, was highly valued by Hasidim. At one point the rebbe dug his hand into the rich rice kugel, and instead of offering it to one of his Hasidim he turned around and offered it to the man in the white suit. Surprised, the man hesitated, but the rebbe, smiling winsomely, urged him, "Take it, take it. I have clean hands" (with an emphasis on "clean hands").

Reb Ahrale devoted much of his time to young people who had strayed from the traditional path. They were attracted by his extraordinary charm, vitality, and directness. Some of his older and affluent Hasidim felt neglected and left him. His brother and rival once called him crazy, to which he responded, "I, who help young Jews find their way back to Judaism, am crazy, whereas my brother, who spends his time with old Jews who will never stray, he is sane."

Shavuoth, which we now celebrate as the holiday of receiving the Torah, was in biblical times a pilgrimage festival. Hasidim combined the two by making a pilgrimage to their rebbe to celebrate the holiday with him. On Shavuoth of 1939 I decided to visit Reb Ahrale. I left the yeshiva after the holiday meal, but at the rebbe's court the throng of Hasidim who had come to celebrate the holiday were still waiting for him to finish the nap after the mikvah. Late in the evening when most Jews had already finished the holiday meal, the rebbe of Kozhenitz, true to his unpredictable self, was still napping while his Hasidim were sitting in small groups and recounting the miracles performed by the rebbes of the Kozhenitzer dynasty, including the present rebbe.

Suddenly there was a surge of activity in the area where the rebbe was resting. The rebbe and his retinue of young Hasidim were getting up from their nap. They joined the Hasidim who were waiting, and soon the woods were resounding with prayers. I stood near the rebbe and was surprised that in the middle of the prayers he was cheerfully chatting with his disciples. One of the Hasidim later explained to me that the rebbe had the ability to transpose mundane conversations into hymns of praise to God. The letters of the Hebrew alphabet also have numeric value; it was therefore possible to change letters to numbers and then create new letters that combined into words with a sacred meaning. It took Hasidic devotion to view the rebbe's ebullience in these terms. I was prepared to believe that this was possible, but I was skeptical about its ability to make a fervent prayer.

Shavuoth, being the holiday that commemorates the revelation at Sinai, was celebrated with a tikkun of studying Torah through the first night. After maarib the rebbe retired to his study. Wanting to know what he was doing, I pulled myself up to the ledge of his window and saw that he was studying Talmud. Outside the Hasidim were sitting in small groups chatting.

Long past midnight the rebbe came out and invited the Hasidim to enter for kiddush. Before kiddush the rebbe donned the venerated cloak that was worn by the founder of the dynasty, Reb Israel, the maggid of Kozhenitz. At that moment, as if infused with new vitality, his face suddenly changed. It became serene and radiant as he chanted the kiddush. When I was returning to the yeshiva the sun was rising. The fiery red of the May sun on the eastern horizon resembled the illumined face of the rebbe during kiddush.

Reb Shaul Yedidya Taub, the Rebbe of Modzhits

Modzhits melodies were the pride and joy of Polish Hasidim. They sang zmirot and prayers to the tunes composed by the rebbes of Modzhits, Reb Shaul Yedidya and his father, Reb Israel. Their shorter nigunim were usually cheerful and rhythmic and were called *marshel*, a diminutive of *march*. The longer ones had several parts that corresponded to the variety of tempos in classical music. When Reb Asher, the Friday night prayer leader at Reb Yosele's, came to "Lekha Dodi," the hymn welcoming the Sabbath Bride, there was a moment of silent expectation: What new Modzhits marshel would he choose? At home we sang the Shabbat zmirot to the tune of Modzhits melodies. Before I went away to the yeshiva I hardly knew any other nigunim. Years later when I began to listen to classical music, I realized that I had been prepared for it by Modzhits nigunim.

Reb Shaul Yedidya, the second Modzhits rebbe, was undoubtedly the most prolific composer of nigunim. He spent summers in Otwock, and on Shavuoth of 1939 I went to his Tish. A long row of tables was set up in the large Beit HaMidrash, but it was only large enough to seat the most distinguished Hasidim. The rest stood around the table several people deep.

To make sure that I would have a good view, I climbed up on the bimah and placed myself directly opposite the rebbe. From there I had a commanding view of the whole Beit HaMidrash. The rebbe was then middle-aged and somewhat stocky; his salt-and-pepper beard and large, penetrating eyes gave him a leonine appearance.

About the middle of the meal, the rebbe tapped his silver snuffbox with his finger and the whole Beit HaMidrash fell silent. After a moment he began to sing a new nigun. The composition consisted of four parts: the first and third were meditative, while the second and fourth were rhythmic and cheerful. The singing was pure melody without words, and the Hasidim who stood behind the rebbe's chair supported him. They sounded like a powerful and well-trained choir. The effect was spellbinding. When they finished the nigun I felt as though I had awakened from a marvelous dream. The singing seemed to have lasted longer than it really did.

On the second day of Shavuoth I visited Reb Yitzhaq Zelik, the Sokolover rebbe. Having been raised in an environment that was strongly influenced by the teachings of Reb Menahem Mendel of Kotzk, I was eager to meet one of his descendants. I was struck by his informality. Tish was a formal event at which the rebbe usually wore a *shtrimel* (a round fur hat), but Reb Yitzhaq Zelik just wore his yarmulke. During the few minutes that I was there he raised seven questions about the first verse of the Book of Ruth and went on to discuss them. After a few minutes I left. It was all too rational, and I was looking for a characteristically Hasidic experience.

On my way back to the yeshiva I stopped to visit the Purisover rebbe, and I was startled by what I saw. A young man about my age sat at the head of the table surrounded by venerable-looking older Hasidim. His father, the previous rebbe of Purisov, had died recently, and the son had been chosen to succeed him. Hasidic leadership was dynastic, and I knew that such things happened, but I'd never seen it firsthand. The sight of a barefaced youth at the head of the table and elders sitting before him with awe was incongruous. The young rebbe had large, bovine eyes and was staring into the distance. Looking at him, I thought of a calf. After puzzling at the sight for a few minutes, I left. When I think about my reaction, I realize how strongly I was influenced by my father's critical view of Hasidism.

Reb Yaakov Yosef, the Lubavitcher Rebbe

Lubavitch is an old Hasidic dynasty; it had a large following in Lithuania and Russia, but few if any adherents in central Poland. Shlomo Singer from my hometown was the first Lubavitch Hasid I knew. He was several years older than I. We never had a conversation, but I remember him from the way he prayed. Long after we had finished our prayers, Shlomo was still standing motionless, not even swaying, his eyes closed, completely absorbed in his prayers. That was my introduction to Lubavitch Hasidism. While I was in Otwock I decided to visit the court of the Lubavitcher on Yob Tamuz, the twelfth day of Tamuz, which celebrates the release of Reb Shneur Zalman, the founder of their dynasty, from a czarist prison in the summer of 1810.

Everything about the Lubavitch court—the rebbe, his Hasidim, the quarters, even the furniture—was different from what I had seen at other Hasidic courts in Poland. The rebbe lived in a beautiful villa in the woods. First I examined the grounds and peeked into windows. The books in the rebbe's library were beautifully bound and neatly stacked on the shelves. Inside the villa I saw for the first time roll-top desks that were used by his male secretaries. In the early afternoon two men in Western dress stood reciting the silent prayer of minhah. They didn't sway like Hasidim; they just stood rapt in prayer much longer than what I was accustomed to.

The celebration took place in a large room in which the table was set with wines, soft drinks, and baked goods, elegantly displayed. The people seated at the table were all distinguished rabbis and Hasidim; the rest stood around them, several people deep. I made my way to a place opposite the rebbe and riveted my eyes on him. Because he had suffered a mild stroke it was difficult to hear him, but his facial expressions were so vivid that they made his speech comprehensible.

During his discourse several students from his yeshiva stood behind his chair serving as recorders. They listened intently, and after a while they left and were replaced by another group. Outside they dictated verbatim to the copiers what the rebbe had said. By the time the discourse was finished, copies of it were already hectographed and available to the Hasidim.

I left feeling that I had witnessed a new and far more complex, ordered, and demanding Hasidism than I had previously known. I have no way of knowing how this experience might have affected me, because within a few months we were living under German occupation.

14

Musarnikes

The Musar movement, founded by Rabbi Israel Salanter in Lithuania in the middle of the nineteenth century, was dedicated to deepening moral sensitivity in religious practice and in personal relations. Rabbi Yosef Yoizl Hurwitz, one of Salanter's disciples, developed the educational theory of the movement and founded yeshivas that applied it. During the 1930s the Beis-Yosef yeshivas, named after him, spread from Lithuania to Poland and became the largest network of yeshivas there. The students of these yeshivas were called Novardiker, after the name of the town where the first yeshiva was located, or Musarnikes, derived from the word *musar* (ethics). In this chapter I recollect impressions of Musarnikes I had encountered.

Yosel Pietrikover, a subdued and sober fellow of just sixteen, seemed older. The thick lenses of his glasses were like a partition through which he saw us. Yosel kept to himself; there was an air of resignation about him that led me to think he had a story to tell. He came to Rahev, where I was studying, after having spent two years at a Beis-Yosef yeshiva in Piotrekov. His father, having noticed a decline in his piety, suspected that he had come under the influence of secularists, something that was common during the 1930s in Poland. To prevent such a calamitous possibility, his father put him under the tutelage of the Musarnikes, who had a reputation for curbing youthful tempers. Many years later, Ezra Perkal, a friend of mine, told me that his father took his fastidiousness in dress as a sign of modernity and sent him off to the Musar yeshiva in Ostrovce (Ostrowiec). In Ezra's case it was too late, but Yosel apparently came to the Musarnikes in the nick of time.

It was from Yosel that I learned about the ways of Musarnikes, including their pensive melodies, some of which I still remember. Novardok differed from other yeshivas by emphasizing, in addition to Talmud and Codes, the study and contemplation of ethical literature. They also engaged in exercises that were designed to curb lust, arrogance, and indolence and to nurture graciousness, fearlessness, and generosity. They worked especially hard to free themselves from the influence of *die gas* (the street)—that is, views that prevailed outside the yeshiva.

One of their slogans was "A mentsch darf arbeten of zich" ("A person has to work on himself"). When they worked on generosity they would carry the buckets for the water carriers or assist the infirm in shopping and crossing the street. To fight indolence they would rise in winter before dawn and run several miles. To become indifferent to public opinion they would do ridiculous things like go to an apothecary with a bucket to purchase ten cents' worth of iodine. Their radical behavior seemed heroic and appealed to teenage yeshiva students.

I first met Musarnikes at home. It was in the early 1930s, and I was about ten. I had come home for the midday meal and, to my surprise, there were visitors: Reb Yitzhoq Shershever, head of the Beis-Yosef yeshiva in Ostrovce, accompanied by two of his older students, had come to call on my father. He brought greetings from Reb Yeshayeh Shpigel, a prosperous hardware merchant in

Ostrovce, whom my father saw annually on Yom Kippur during visits to the rebbe of Suchedniov. The Musarnikes had opened a yeshiva in Ostrovce and were looking for support in Radom, the largest city of the district. They hoped that my father, who was a highly regarded communal leader, could help them.

This was during the depression, and I don't know what my father was able to do for the yeshiva, but that visit started a friendship between them. Several years later, when I was a student in Rahev, the preparatory of the famous Yeshiva Hakhmei Lublin, my father asked me to stop over in Ostrovce and visit Reb Yitzhoq on my way home for Passover. My father, who was a religious man and quite a Talmudist, had little traffic with the Klei Kodesh—the "Holy Vessels," as rabbis and religious functionaries were derogatorily called in Poland—but there were always exceptions, and Reb Yitzhoq was one of them.

Equipped with what I had learned from Yosel about the Novardiker, I went to Ostrovce, the largest Musar yeshiva in central Poland. What struck me first was the shabbiness of the place and the appearance of the students. Musarnikes were indifferent to externalities, whether physical surroundings or personal attire. They were serious to the point of being grim except when they were celebrating a holiday or a wedding, when their suppressed gaiety would burst into full play.

Reb Itzhoq was glad to see me and invited me home for lunch. His home consisted of one room divided by a white bedsheet. Behind it was the bedroom with an infant, his firstborn. His wife wasn't home, and he didn't bother to explain. The meal was ample but plain: meatloaf and potatoes. Reb Itzhoq apologized for not receiving me more lavishly, as would befit the son of his distinguished friend. He didn't know that at home we ate no better, the depression having reduced my father's business so that even meatloaf was hard to come by.

When we parted he gave me several issues of *Hayey Hamusar* (*The Life of Musar*), a moralistic journal that he edited. On the bus I thumbed through some of them; the journals, like the Musarnikes, were grim. One of the stories was about two people who came to a rabbi with a dispute over a plot of land that each of them claimed. The rabbi listened to their claims, then took them to the plot, went down on his knees, cocked his ear to the ground, and after a moment of attentive listening got up and told the disputants, "I hear the ground saying that both of you belong to her."

From Ostrovce I went to Driltch, a little town in the vicinity of Radom, to visit Rachmiel, my sister's fiancée. Driltch was a typical shtetl populated mostly by Jews. From that visit I remember only two things, and both were connected with the Novardiker. In the morning Rachmiel and I went to pray at the Beit HaMidrash. During the prayers I heard a heart-rending wailing coming from the women's section, which was connected to the main room by windows. The wailing went on and on; I was sure someone had died, but I couldn't understand why the family didn't mourn at home. When I could no longer contain myself, I asked Rachmiel, "Who died?" Rachmiel looked at me surprised and said, "Nobody. These are the wailings of Musarnikes studying Musar *behislives* [with fervor]." The Musarnikes would whip themselves into a high emotional state by chanting, over and over again, moral phrases from biblical or rabbinic texts that pointed to human failings until they would break down into weeping. Rachmiel then explained that during Elul, the month preceding the High Holidays, the Musarnikes left the city to study Musar. They began the day at dawn meditating in the woods, and when they returned they studied Musar at the women's section of the Beit HaMidrash. What I had heard was just a fervent Musar session.

Later in the day when we returned for the evening prayers, two Musarnikes addressed the congregation during the break between minhah and maarib—the afternoon and evening prayers. Standing in front of the Ark, they made an appeal for community support of the Beis-Yosef yeshiva they were establishing in Driltch. They had it all worked out: they would provide the teachers, and the women's section of the Beit HaMidrash, which was not used during the week, would be their classroom. They were asking the *balebatim* (householders) to provide food and lodging for out-of-town students. That was how two Musarnikes of about fifteen years of age established a new yeshiva. They seemed not to have the slightest doubt about what they proposed; they were convinced that it was right and beneficial to the townspeople, and they persuasively conveyed this conviction to them. Within half an hour, enough people had volunteered to take care of the prospective students and the founding meeting was over. I was impressed by their poise, self-confidence, courage, convictions, and eloquence. I couldn't imagine having the courage to do what they did. What I saw was an example of Musarnik training at work.

Back home in Radom, I met Reb Shmuel Yanover, a Musarnik from the Bialystok yeshiva who had come to live in our town. He spoke Yiddish with a Lithuanian accent, and like Lithuanian yeshiva students, he wore a regular suit and hat. He was small and lean, just skin and bones, but he had an intense, austere expression on his face. He was a man of few words, restrained yet cordial. He spoke deliberately, his coal-black eyes looking intently at you. One sensed that the man was in full control of himself and that his behavior was not random but the result of long cultivation.

The Musarnik who left an indelible impression on me was Reb Berl. He came to live in Radom because he had married into a local family and was on Kest. Reb Berl had set himself up in the Kozhenitzer shtibl, although he was not a follower of that rebbe (like most Lithuanians, he was not a Hasid). It was a matter of convenience: the shtibl was near to his in-laws' house and was empty except for morning and evening prayers. In that shtibl he prayed and studied, and in the evening his wife would bring him supper. That is also where he slept, on a bare bench. The only time he slept at home was on Shabbat, when even a scholar is obliged to fulfill his conjugal duty. In no time Reb Berl became a legend. Yeshiva students reported his great fervor during prayer, his diligence in learning, and his saintly behavior. He lived by ideals of piety that we admired but lacked the strength to practice.

One day, as I was walking with my friend Zvi Kaner, I noticed a man walking briskly off the sidewalk, his head lowered and his eyes looking down in front of him. It struck me that this man was complying with several austere dicta in the Talmud: "Better walk behind a lion than behind a woman"; "One should not walk between two women"; and, in awareness of God's presence, "One should not walk with an upraised head." Looking at him, I asked Zvi, "Is this Reb Berl?" and he nodded. At that moment the legend became real and I decided to meet him.

Friday of that week, on my way to the mikvah, I went to visit Reb Berl. As I was walking up the steps to the Kozhenitzer shtibl I felt uncomfortable: I was about to disturb a saintly person to satisfy my curiosity. I was also afraid that a man who is so strict with himself might be annoyed by my intrusion. I entered the shtibl as if I had come to look up something in its library. I went directly to the bookshelves, pulled out books, looked at them briefly, and replaced them, until I was near him. Reb Berl was studying and paid no attention to me.

Finally, I approached him. In response to my greetings, he raised his head, and his large, gray eyes were disarmingly friendly. His unexpected reaction left me speechless. I simply didn't know what to say to him. I looked down and saw that he was studying the laws of business in the Code of Reb Josef Caro, and I asked him, "Why are you studying the laws of business?" He responded as if my question was entirely appropriate. "I will tell you: my wife is pregnant. When I become a father I will have to support my family. I have no trade so I will have to engage in business. I am therefore studying the laws of business so that I know what is permissible and what is forbidden in business dealings." All the while he was talking he looked at me with his large, friendly eyes, speaking as though I was his friend of long ago. That image of him has remained with me.

15

Bathya's Engagement

One day, shortly after I had turned eight, I came home for lunch, burst into the living room, and was surprised to see a beautiful young woman of about twenty sitting at the table before a mirror. She wore lipstick, something that traditional girls, including my sisters, frowned upon. She greeted me with the question, "Yingele, vus lernstu?" ("Little boy, what are you studying?"). I answered, "Gemore" ("Talmud"). I had just begun to study Talmud and was proud of it. To my surprise, the young lady proceeded to examine me. There was something odd about it. Women usually didn't study Talmud. Then, there was an air of worldliness about her which didn't suggest that she would spend her time studying Talmud.

When I talked to my mother I discovered that Bathya was the daughter of the rabbi of Premislan, a little town in eastern Galicia. She was about to become engaged to the grandson of the Hasidic rebbe of Suchedniov. Since my father was a friend of the rebbe and his family, it was decided that she would stay with us, and the young man would stay in the home of another of his grandfather's followers.

Of course you realize that this was an arranged match and the prospective bride and groom had only heard from the shadchan about each other, or better yet, of their distinguished families. The couple was brought together so that they see each other, as is required by Jewish law. Toward evening, the party of the groom arrived. The groom, surrounded by several men, was dressed in rabbinical garb. I had a good look at him: he was tall with hunched shoulders, thick spectacles, and a long, red nose. His nearsightedness made him look foolish. And I thought, What? He is going to marry this beautiful woman? Though I was a little boy, I felt that the match was incongruous.

A few months later my father received a letter from Bathya, written in beautiful modern Hebrew, informing him that she had broken her engagement with the rebbe's grandson and was marrying the son of the town's apothecary. In small towns the Jewish intelligentsia was usually led by the physician and the apothecary, both of whom had a higher secular education.

16

Love's First Glance

I met Avrum Yehiel by chance, while I was going somewhere with my father. I was impressed by the way they enjoyed seeing each other. While they were talking I had the opportunity to observe Avrum Yehiel. He was a handsome, middle-age man of medium height with an olive-complexioned, oval face. His hair and beard were so black that they had a tinge of deep blue. His eyes sparkled, and when he smiled his whole face lit up. Avrum Yehiel knew how to live comfortably in different environments. He was a Hasid and a talmid chacham, a learned man, who earned his livelihood representing hardware companies. On weekdays, when he was engaged in business, he wore a Western-type short jacket instead of the traditional capote.

After the Germans occupied Poland, one of their earliest decrees was to prohibit Jewish public worship and education. Avrum Yehiel invited a group of yeshiva students to study and worship in his large apartment. At first we met there only on Shabbat.

One Shabbat morning before the services, I was sitting at a table reviewing the Torah portion of the week. Across the table from me sat Rachmiel Briks. Though we were members of the same group of young talmudists, I looked up to him. He was only a couple of years older than I, but Rachmiel had already studied at the famous Lublin yeshiva, whereas I had only studied in its preparatory school. I noticed that he was reading the Zohar, the mystical commentary on the Bible written in Aramaic that traditional Jews called the Holy Zohar. I asked him, "Rachmiel, do you understand the Zohar?" and he replied, "No." "Then why do you read it?" He answered, "It inspires piety." His answer struck me as strange. Apparently, I was already then more of a rationalist than I suspected.

Of Avrum Yechiel's family I remember his son Kalman and his daughter Rachel. Kalman, Avrum Yechiel's firstborn, was frail and mentally not up to his age, but cheerful and friendly. Rachel was an attractive young woman of seventeen. Her well-proportioned face with high cheekbones and large, green gray eyes commanded one's attention. I had noticed Rachel and was drawn to her, but I had never spoken with her. Among Hasidim, young men and women did not converse before they were engaged.

Shortly after our study group had moved into Avrum Yechiel's apartment, Kalman became ill and after a couple weeks he died. It so happened that he died late on Friday afternoon. In Poland we didn't have funeral parlors that could be called to remove a body, so when we arrived for the Friday night service his body was on the floor, covered with a sheet.

On Saturday afternoon at shalosh seudot, the prescribed third meal of Shabbat, Avrum Yechiel joined us as usual. When we sang zmirot, the Shabbat hymns, he sang louder than usual; there was a suppressed scream in his voice, but he sang. Shabbat was not to be overcome by mourning.

A couple of months later we found out that some members of our group were suffering from hunger because their parents could no longer provide them with food. Without hesitation, Avrum Yehiel invited us to establish a soup kitchen in his apartment. Out of solidarity with the less fortunate members of our group, several of us who still had food at home would join in these meals. Avrum Yechiel's wife and daughter prepared the food and cleaned the dishes and pots.

One day as I was leaving I passed Rachel, who was rinsing a rather large soup kettle. To see me she had turned her head and the upper part of her body away from the sink, unwittingly creating a provocative profile. Our eyes met in a lingering glance. I felt as though I had been singled out.

That encounter revealed to me, for the first time, my approaching adulthood and the possibility of an affectionate relationship with a woman. In normal times, considering the friendly relations between our parents, it is likely that within a couple of years our silent romance would have led to marriage. Alas, we were living under German occupation. A couple of years later our families were murdered by the Germans. Only I survived. Though sixty years have passed, I remember that encounter vividly.

17

Escape to Freedom

On April 23, 1945, the U.S. Army liberated me from the prison of Ulm, on the Danube, in southwest Germany. This ended the most tragic and painful five years in my life and in the history of our people. How I, a young Jew from Poland, came to the prison of Ulm is a long story, which I will tell in some detail. But first I want to relate two episodes.

Several weeks after the Germans marched into Radom in September 1939, one of their units set up an auto repair shop in the courtyard of our apartment building. I was then sixteen, inquisitive and full of self-confidence. Cars were rare in Poland, and I was curious about them. I was even more curious about the Germans, and now both were right there under my nose. The German mechanics seemed less threatening in their fatigues than in uniform. Passing by them, I would stop and watch for a while until one of them noticed me and muttered some words in my direction, the way a busy mechanic comments without interrupting his work. Encouraged by his civility, I returned to watch him work.

About that time, the Germans had issued a decree that Jews must take their hats off when they encounter German soldiers.

To preserve my dignity, I decided to turn this into a real greeting, sometimes eliciting a friendly response. One day, when I stopped to watch the mechanic, he suddenly shouted at me, "Mitze ap!" ("Hat off!"). I was startled by his unexpected demand; it even struck me as funny to receive such an order from a grease monkey. I looked at him puzzled, and started to giggle. Suddenly he dropped his work and approached me menacingly. I fled, and he chased me for a while, but I was fleet and he couldn't catch me. Eventually he became winded and had to give up. From then on I made sure to avoid that part of our courtyard.

The second episode took place shortly after I was transferred into Germany, in the summer of 1944. It was the first day at work. We were building a huge underground structure and were guarded by Germans. Many of the workers were Russians who had been shipped to Germany to replace the Germans who had been sent to the front. We, the concentration camp prisoners, were brought to do the heavy support work. That day, I was unloading a trainload of iron reinforcement rods and distributing them to the workers who were shaping them. While working, I nicked my forehead and it bled. As I passed a group of Russian workers, one of them, a young woman, ran to the office and got a bandage. When I passed her again she stopped me, and while applying the bandage she told me to meet her at noon. When we met she gave me some bread. I, deeply moved, wanted to tell her, "Enough!" But instead of saying "dovolno," which means "enough" in Russian, I kept saying "dai," which means "enough" in Hebrew, but in Russian it means "give"! The contradiction between my tone and the meaning of what I said must have been puzzling to her. That young woman managed to spare food for me throughout the months I was in that camp. Her generosity may have meant the difference between life and death for me.

After liberation I went to every trainload of Russians being repatriated, looking for her, but I never found her.

Now to the story of my escape. During March 1945, I was in the concentration camp of Kochendorf. The U.S. Army had pushed the Germans back into Germany, and the front lines were close enough to our camp. In the quiet of the night we could hear the thud of exploding artillery shells and felt encouraged. At the next distribution of clothing, I was thinking about the possibility of escape, I chose a regular jacket marked on the back with a wide column of red instead of the usual concentration camp striped one.

On March 29 we were awakened before dawn, lined up, counted, and marched out of the camp with our blankets under our arms. Our destination was Dachau, the concentration camp of which our camp was a branch.

That morning each of us received a somewhat larger portion of bread that was to last us through the day. But I couldn't contain myself, and eating my portion a few bites at a time, I finished it in about an hour. Shortly after the beginning of the march, one of the guards ordered me to carry his knapsack. Toward evening we were herded into a fenced-in field where we were to spend the night. The guard whose knapsack I was carrying lost sight of me and failed to claim it. After it became dark I covered myself with the blanket, opened the knapsack, and took out a fortune: two whole loaves of bread. This was the most I had at one time in two years. I abandoned the knapsack, divided the loaves with my neighbor, and we began to eat. We had to finish it before dawn. My saliva gave out and, having no water, the chewing became more and more difficult. Though I had lost the taste of the bread, I continued to chew until it was finished.

Early in the morning we were lined up again and marched off. As soon as the sun was up, British airplanes flew over us and the guards took cover in the woods near the road. When the planes returned, the guards ordered us into the woods and decided to march us during the night. That whole day we lay in a clearing and enjoyed the sight of the guards cowering every time the planes flew over the area. Toward evening we were lined up again and marched off.

Late that night I volunteered to push one of the wagons that went with us on the march. Some of wagons carried the guards' knapsacks and the meager provisions for the prisoners, while others carried the corpses of prisoners who had died from exhaustion on the way. Pushing along with others helped to keep me awake. From time to time I dozed off while holding onto the wagon.

At dawn we camped in a clearing in the woods. The ground was wet from dew, and edible berries had been preserved by the winter's frost. In no time the berries directly under us disappeared. They were juicy and refreshing after the night's march. I was crawling along in search of berries and must have gone a bit away from the camp when I received a boot in the coccyx that I remembered for a long time.

The next night I was too weak to continue marching and decided to play dead so that I would be loaded onto one of the wagons. As soon as I dropped onto the road, I was picked up and thrown among the corpses. Soon a corpse was thrown on top of me, and to free myself I jerked part of my body. The nearby guard noticed it and brought down his heavy stick over the wagon to finish off the dying. Fortunately, it didn't reach me. Toward dawn, when we camped and the corpses were unloaded, I crawled away and joined the rest of the prisoners.

That day was rainy, and we were put up in several hay barns. I remember lying in a daze, with a buzzing in my ears. In my hallucination I saw clocks and wristwatches. Toward evening, when we lined up, the camp doctor felt each prisoner's pulse and separated the weak from the strong. I was among the weak. We received a bit of food and, for the first time, a pack of cigarettes. We lined up five abreast: the healthy marched first and the weak followed, marching arm in arm to support each other.

That night I was overcome by the feeling that unless I managed to escape, it would be my last night. Suddenly, a military convoy came onto the road and marched side by side with us so that we were pressed to the far right of the road. Trudging along, I desperately looked for an escape. I even thought of jumping on one of the wagons. Suddenly I noticed that not far ahead, maybe some fifty yards, the road took a sharp turn to the right. A house stood at the corner, blocking the view so that the guard on the right, having turned, couldn't look back. I realized that if I managed to escape at the turn of the road, I might succeed. Quickly I disengaged myself from the arm of the fellow holding on to me, moved over to the right, pushed the other four to the left, and marched along for a moment. As soon as the guard ahead of me turned right, I looked back and couldn't see the guard behind me. The fence of the house was low; I flipped over it and covered myself with my dark gray blanket.

I lay there listening to the convoy until I could no longer hear it. I tried to get up, but my feet wouldn't bear me; they were too shaky, and I fell. The escape seemed to have consumed the residue of my energy. I lay there for a while; then, crawling, I found a stick by which I pulled myself up. I stood leaning on it for a few minutes before I returned to the road. It was about midnight; the village was pitch dark in blackout for fear of air attacks. Looking into the darkness, I noticed a glimmer of light from the opposite side of the road. I went toward it not realizing that the road was separated from the house by a ditch, and I fell right into it. Fortunately, I was only startled, not hurt, and I climbed back onto the road.

It was raining. As I stood there, in the dark, free but alone in Germany, the rain lashing my face, I was overcome by a feeling of helplessness and began to cry. For the first time in years I cried; I never cried in the concentration camp. Soon I composed myself, and, looking intently about me, I again saw a light not too far from where I was standing. For some reason I imagined that it was a barn and the farmer was milking his cows. I approached the place, knocked on the door, and a military policeman opened it. Since he was in the light and I was in the dark, he couldn't see me. He asked what I wanted. I replied, "Food." At first he turned me away, saying he had none; then he called me back into the barn, quickly took my stick away, told me to sit down, and questioned me. I told him that I was exhausted and hungry. He turned the light out, left the barn, and told me that he would soon return.

As soon as he left I got up and began to feel my way around the barn, searching for food. I discovered that someone was sleeping behind the partition, and I decided to leave. When I opened the barn door the military police officer was still standing there. He asked me where I was going, and I replied that I was looking for food. He had been standing in front of the barn, probably wondering what to do with me. Our convoy had passed the village only an hour before, and he must have known who I was. After my last appeal for food, he asked me to follow him. He took me to a crossroads where another officer stood directing traffic, spoke with him, and then called over a village militiaman to take charge of me. I noticed that another prisoner was standing on the opposite side of the road. For a moment it occurred to me that they might shoot both of us, but the militiaman took us to the village prison, unlocked it, and let us in.

The prison consisted of one room with nothing but a bed. There was no light, so both of us lay down to sleep. We talked for a few minutes, and I learned that my prison mate was a young Ukrainian who introduced himself as Kishka-Gut. He got into the concentration camp the honest way, being a professional thief. After two and a half years of sleeping on bare boards, it felt luxurious to sleep on a bed. I remember thanking God for it, and, overcome by weariness, I fell asleep instantly. In the morning I was awakened by Kishka, who had already searched every corner of the prison for food. Not knowing German, he needed my help to speak with the children who were passing by the prison window on their way to school. Most of them were afraid to stop, but I managed to persuade one of them to give us his lunch in exchange for several cigarettes.

Later that morning, the door was unlocked and the same elderly militiaman came to take us to Gaildorf, the nearest district town. I explained to him that we couldn't go until we had something to eat, and he brought us each a large chunk of black bread and a jar of water. We sat on a tree stump outside the prison and ate. People passed us on their way to work; most of them looked away.

Once breakfast was over, we began our march. Along the way we were joined by two other prisoners who apparently had escaped from the convoy. One of them was Janek, who had fought in the Warsaw uprising of 1944; the other was a Ukrainian named Kuznetsov. On the way we were allowed to pick up cigarette butts, invaluable prisoner goodies.

In Gaildorf we were brought to the district police headquarters. While we awaited questioning we were given plenty of food. On that day I probably ate more than at any other time in my life. It was a miracle that I survived it. Sometime during that eating orgy, I told my three colleagues that we should prepare ourselves for the interrogation. Since I was the only one who could speak German, it was decided that I would be the spokesman. It occurred to me that if we told the police that we were all from the same concentration camp, they would send us back to the convoy that had passed the area the night before. I therefore decided that each of us should claim to be from a different concentration camp. Knowing the German penchant for order, I thought this might confuse the police and help us gain time.

When we were called in for questioning and asked who was the spokesman, I came forward. To test the officer's severity I asked for permission to sit down, and he gave it. He then proceeded to question us. My comrades held to their stories, and I invented a story that I was in the concentration camp because I was of mixed parentage, my mother having been a German and my father a Jew. When he heard our stories the officer exclaimed, "Damn. They have me utterly confused!" For the time being my strategy had worked. The officer dismissed us, saying that he was going to find out what to do with us. Meanwhile, we were to remain in the room assigned to us.

Toward evening, the officer returned, called me in, and told me that he had found out what to do with us. There was a convoy of prisoners like us not far from Gaildorf, and he was going to take us there. Realizing that I was again between life and death, I decided not to mince words. I asked him, "Do you know what they will do to us?" He responded, "Look, I didn't make you prisoners; you came to me as such." The fact that he had bothered to justify himself gave me courage, and with tears in my eyes I pleaded, "You may have someone fighting at the front, and you would like him to return home alive. The moment you take us back to the concentration camp convoy the guards will kill us." He replied, "I'm not all-powerful." I continued to plead, "Look, we're all sick. Why don't you take us to the infirmary for the foreign laborers?" He hesitated for a moment, then said, "I'll try. If I don't come at six in the morning, you'll know that I have succeeded."

I returned to the other prisoners. They asked me what had happened, but I saw no point in worrying them and just brushed it off. It was already late in the evening, and we lay down to sleep on the floor. That whole night I lay awake wondering what was going to happen. At dawn I heard someone coming up the stairs; he then came into the room and washed his hands at the sink. As he was leaving I asked him what time it was. "Six fifteen," he replied. I breathed a deep sigh of relief and fell asleep on the spot, or maybe I just passed out. When I was awakened several hours later, the police officer was there; he had come to take us to the infirmary.

The nurse who registered us asked me how old I was. When I gave her my date of birth, she looked surprised and repeated her question. I soon discovered why. I was given shaving gear, and when I looked in the mirror I saw the face of a wizened middle-aged man. My skin was yellow and stretched tightly over the facial bones. My eyes, sunken deep in their sockets like the eyes of a dead skull, were looking at me with terror. This was the first time I'd seen myself in a long time, and I didn't recognize myself. I was twenty-two.

We were left in the infirmary for a couple of days. At night the shooting became louder; the front seemed to be very near. I began to think of hiding out until the town was captured. Then, on the third morning, a policeman came and ordered us to march away with him. He escorted us to the next village and left us with the village policeman. As soon as our escort was gone, I suggested to the aging policeman that instead of escorting us himself he should just give us a certificate stating that we are marching to Allen, the direction we were supposed to be head-ing. I reassured him, saying, "We are in the middle of Germany, and look how we're dressed; there is no way we can escape." He agreed, gave us the document, and sent us off with a warning to be out of town by evening.

Free again, we marched away to the edge of town and began to solicit food from the farmers. That evening I ate so much potato salad that I couldn't eat it again for years. We slept in an open barn and in the morning marched to the next village. The next day was Sunday, I believe Easter Sunday. It occurred to me that I should go to the local pastor and present myself as a former student of theology, in the hope that he might help me. I found him home, introduced myself, and to verify my claim he asked me to recite the beginning of the Bible. I stood there looking at him and couldn't remember words that I'd known ever since I was a child. My memory was blank. In retrospect, I'm less surprised by that failure of memory than by my ability to think clearly about the situation I was in and manipulate it. The pastor gave me breakfast and let me go.

As we were making the rounds of the village collecting food, we were suddenly stopped by a plainclothesman with a handgun directed at us. He inquired what we were doing there. We showed him our document and explained that we were marching to Allen on the order of the police. He accepted our explanation but warned us to clear out of town by evening.

That evening, as we heard the cannons exploding, we decided to hide out in the woods in the vicinity of that village. But the night was cold, and so the next morning we climbed up a hill to warm ourselves by the rising sun and eat the bread we had gathered the day before. As we sat there, the same plainclothesman appeared and ordered us to come down. He escorted us to the next village, ordering the police there to do the same. So we marched for several days, from village to town, spending the nights in prison, until we reached Ulm on the Danube and were put in the town prison.

Two of our escorts I remember for different reasons. One was the policeman who took us to Heidenheim. He didn't speak to us, but by the way he treated us he conveyed a feeling of compassion and sensitivity. He marched us at the speed we chose, and we took our time. At lunchtime he led us by a factory and patiently watched us gather food from the workers. The other was a garrulous old man who marched us to Ulm. When he discovered that I spoke German, he asked me why I was a prisoner, and I repeated my story of mixed parentage being my sin. He reassured me that "When we win the war, you can appeal for clemency, and I am sure that the Führer will take it into consideration." Two weeks before the war ended, there were still true believers.

When we got to Ulm the four of us were put in a small cell at the town prison. Upon entering I was given the number 272. I interpreted it to mean two times seven plus two, sixteen days. Sure enough, that's what happened. After two weeks a battle raged for two days on the outskirts of Ulm. After several hours of silence we heard a noise in the prison: our door opened and we faced American soldiers. These were soldiers direct from battle, but they were stunned by our appearance.

We were now free. The German prisoners went home, but those of us who had nowhere to go made the prison our home. We were fed American K-rations. For the first time I came across Nescafé. I frequently mixed myself strong cups of Nescafé with plenty of sugar, which entirely joggled my worn nervous system. Eating more normally had also upset my stomach, and I was taken to the city hospital to be treated for malnutrition and exhaustion. After two weeks I was discharged and given a room in a private home. Thus began my life as a free man.

I don't remember thinking about my family when I was in the camps. All of my mental and physical energy was focused on surviving. When the war ended I was alone, ill from malnutrition, homeless, and destitute. But I was hoping against hope that some of them had survived. That hope was so powerful that while riding in a Jeep to Stuttgart I had a daydream that I was going to visit my father.

As soon as I regained my health I went to Feldafing, a camp for displaced persons where many people from Radom had gathered after the war. There I learned the grim fate of my family. In 1942 my father and my sister Beila were transported to the extermination camp Treblinka; my father died on the way from a massive heart attack, and Beila was murdered there. In January 1943 my two other sisters and my brother-in-law were also sent to Treblinka. My mother was murdered and burned in Auschwitz in 1944. It was a tragic fate that I shared with most of those who had survived the war.

A year later, I came to the United States and was surrounded by people with families. This intensified my loneliness, and I began to suffer from depression. It didn't help that people were nice to me. I always had to return to myself, to my fears, furies, and anguish. I was in limbo. I remember walking the streets of Philadelphia and being surprised at myself for wishing I hadn't survived the war.

Years later, after I married, had children, and had an absorbing job, I began to grieve. Each holiday when I recite the Yizkor (Memorial Prayers), in which one remembers by name family members who have died, I also recall their faces and their appearance, and I am overcome by a gnawing sadness that lingers. To the present day, when the congregation recites the mourner's Kaddish I close my eyes and recall the face of each member of my family.

18

The Encounter

In the fall of 1953 I came to New York to study at the Jewish Theological Seminary. One afternoon, while on my way to do an errand, I noticed at the gate a man dressed like a Polish rabbi. I went up to him and introduced myself in Yiddish. To my surprise, he responded in the English of a Brooklyn native. At that time I was still looking for surviving relatives and friends. I told him that I was from Radom, Poland. He told me that Moishe and Zelig Neiman and Shmulik Margulis from my town had survived and were his neighbors. Within an hour, the time it took him to get home, they called inviting me to visit them at their diamond-polishing business on Forty-seventh Street in Manhattan.

The three of them knew me from the yeshiva. Under the Nazis we had worked together running an underground heder. We also saw each other at Avrum Yechiel's apartment, a secret shtibl where yeshiva fellows met to pray and study. Though I was several years younger, they considered me one of them.

I rang the bell of their shop, and when the door opened the three of them were there waiting for me. They looked just as they did before the war, with beards and peyes and large velvet yarmulkes; my head was uncovered. Shmulik, who was closest to me and had admired my father, upon seeing me without a yarmulke, barely greeted me. After a few minutes of exchanging information about how each of us survived, Zelig called me into his office and offered me money. When I refused he was surprised and asked, "Then why do you go to Schechters?" (that's how Orthodox Jews referred to the seminary). As I was leaving, Shmulik, who was a sharp Kozhenitzer Hasid, shouted after me, "Bentzeyen! You are on the way to becoming a pickpocket!"

A week later I got a call from Zelig inviting me for Shabbat. Friday during the long subway ride I wondered why I had accepted the invitation. I suppose our common past still had a hold on me; besides, I was alone and there was a whiff of home about them.

Zelig's wife, an attractive American woman of about thirty, greeted me at the door. Her head was covered with a scarf in the manner of ultra-Orthodox women. I had forgotten that in their circles one does not shake hands with women. My hand remained for a moment in the air while she looked at me with apprehension, but her cordial greeting diminished the embarrassment. Behind her was a little girl of five or six—Ruchele; she and I quickly became friends. Soon Zelig came home, emptied his pockets, took a shower, and we went to *daven* (pray).

This was the first time in thirteen years that I was in a Hasidic place of worship. It seemed much longer: the time I had spent in concentration camps couldn't be measured by normal months and years. I stood with my back to the window observing, with the detachment of an ethnographer, and comparing what I saw with what I knew from before the war. There was the same sour smell of the towel over the water barrel, the same pacing up and down during prayer, the same swaying back and forth, the same sudden bursts of loud and emphatic prayer, the same ecstatic clapping of hands. The only thing that was different was that I wasn't one of them.

We came home. Zelig made kiddush. During the meal he kept trying to bring me back to my former self. He persisted until I told him, "Zelig, both of us have studied in the yeshiva, so you ought to know that my choice was not made out of ignorance. There is no point in arguing. If we are to remain friends you will have to respect my choice as I respect yours." Zelig didn't try again.

We sang zmirot, and Ruchele sat next to me and enjoyed my attention. While reaching for a plate she accidentally touched one of the candlesticks, something that is prohibited on Shabbat. Zelig sternly exclaimed, "Ruchele!" and her face expressed fear and apprehension as though she had touched a taboo. That put an end to her playfulness.

The next day was uneventful. We went to the same shtibl. The midday meal was cordial but with little conversation. Zelig had realized that he couldn't sway me. Apparently, that was his main reason for inviting me. I never heard from him again.

19

After Liberation

In 1939 I was a Hasidic youth of sixteen deeply rooted in the Jewish tradition and confident in my beliefs. In 1945, after six years in the ghetto and in concentration camps, I was in a state of physical and emotional exhaustion and spiritual numbness. Along with the loss of my family and my people, I had also lost two important sources of stability and comfort: the belief in divine providence and the belief in the goodness of human beings. The destruction of the largest and most devout Jewish community in modern history undermined my belief in divine justice, and my experiences in concentration camps led me to conclude that human beings are potentially the most dangerous creatures on earth.

The process of going from religious commitment to religious confusion began when I was still in the ghetto. I remember a particular event that made prayer difficult for me. In the spring of 1941 we were living in a ghetto and were periodically harassed or beaten. One day a rumor spread that the Germans were planning an "action" against Communists ("action" was a euphemism for murder). In the middle of the night we heard shots, and my father and I went into hiding. There was a tile factory in the courtyard of our apartment building that belonged to the Kozlowsky family, who were Poles. With their knowledge we hid in a large, empty oven where tiles were fired. In the morning, after the shooting had stopped, we returned home.

My father and I were getting ready to recite the morning prayers when there was a knock on the door. It was the sister of Itche Glikler. Her brother had been murdered, and she came to ask my father, who was a member of the Jewish Help Committee, to help them get Itche a grave of his own. Itche was a young man whom we all admired for his learning, piety, and sensitivity. I was particularly fond of him, and the idea that he had been shot in the gutter as a Communist was shattering.

After his sister left I returned to the morning prayers, but as I recited the opening verse, "Hodu La'adonai, kir'u vishmo hodiu va'amim ali'lotav" ("Give thanks to the Lord, call upon His name; make known His deeds among the nations"), the words stuck in my throat. Until this experience my problem with prayer was my tendency to daydream; at times I failed to focus on what I was saying. This time I couldn't pray because I understood what I was saying. I repeated the verse several times, but I couldn't go on. I took off the *tefillin* and sat there stunned. Several hours later, just before the appointed time for morning prayers was about to end, I put the tefillin on again and recited the prayers quickly, the way one runs through a mine field. I need not tell you that my subsequent experiences in the concentration camps didn't improve my ability to pray.

For several years after my liberation, even when I was already in the United States, I was still in a state of confusion. I didn't know how to think about God, what to do about prayer. At the same time, I continued to have a strong attachment to the Jewish way of life: its traditions, its holidays and festivals, its rituals, and its literature. It was my culture, but under the radically altered circumstances of my life I didn't know how to give expression to it. In college one of my professors, also a Jew, once asked me, "Mr. Gold, I know that you are not observant, so why don't you come to class on Saturdays and on Jewish holidays?" I replied, "What I do with my tradition privately is a personal matter, but violating it publicly would be a declaration that it did not matter." I was in the odd situation of being in exile from God but at home with the Jewish tradition, and not knowing what to do about it. I was then a Hebrew teacher, and I taught the children Jewish traditions with warmth and conviction, but at Shabbat services I read Midrash instead of praying.

Several things impeded the healing of my alienation. One was that I had an unrealistic sense of the Judaism that we practiced in Poland before the war. Celebrations of Shabbat and holidays in the United States paled by comparison with my memories of the way our family had observed them. I had exaggerated their beauty and meaningfulness to the point that no observance in the present could match them. Then there was my thinking about Judaism in the simplistic terms of my childhood. After that terrible tragedy I was still looking for the certainty of a Hasidic youth in Poland.

I was teaching Hebrew at a conservative congregation, but having grown up in an Orthodox home precluded the possibility of becoming a Conservative Jew. How could I take seriously what I had grown up to view as compromised? At the same time, when I tried an Orthodox synagogue I didn't feel like I belonged there either. I was comparing an idealized past with a prejudged present.

I had learned English rather quickly, and I seemed to be a "regular fellow." Few people knew, and I'm not sure that even I realized, what was going on inside me. In Poland my education was strictly within the Jewish tradition. In heder I had learned a little Polish, history, and arithmetic. In the yeshiva we viewed all secular education as contaminating. We actually believed that we had nothing to learn from the goyim. It was in the United States that I first became acquainted with Western literature. I read the works of Tolstoy, Dostoyevsky, and Voltaire, and was impressed by them. I also read the classics of modern Hebrew and Yiddish literature, and their critique of the life I had lived before the war was not lost on me. All of these factors affected me deeply. I was a battleground of conflicting ideas and loyalties that contended for my allegiance and were shaping my new self.

The turning point came when I had to decide what I was going to do with my life. I was then living in Chicago and supported myself from teaching in a Conservative congregation. At college I had studied education and anthropology. At the same time, I was also working on a doctorate in Hebrew literature at the College of Jewish Studies. When I asked myself what was really important to me, I got a clear answer. Three things were important to me: Jews, Judaica (that is, Jewish learning), and Judaism (the practice of the Jewish tradition). After the Holocaust, as far as I was concerned, the only cultural and religious tradition that was unsullied was Judaism. It didn't take me long to realize that these three interests could be fulfilled only in the rabbinate.

This finding presented me with a new dilemma. Feeling alienated from God and unable to accept the traditional doctrine of reward and punishment, how could I think of becoming a rabbi? True, I had an attachment to the traditional way of life, but I had lived without it long enough to make me wonder whether my attachment was nostalgic or real. While I couldn't resolve this dilemma, I was sure of one thing: I had a longing for the study of Talmud, I suppose because this was the link to my prewar self. On the strength of this realization I applied for admission to the Jewish Theological Seminary. I am grateful to the leaders of the seminary, particularly to professors Louis Finkelstein, Simon Greenberg, and Abraham Joshua Heschel, who interviewed me. They saw my perplexities and my inability to commit to becoming a rabbi, but nonetheless they accepted me to the seminary.

In retrospect, I'm glad I had the courage to make that decision, because it led to wrestling with my doubts while I was engaged in the study of traditional Jewish sources. Without my immersion in them, I might have ended up like many Jews who started where I was. Like them, I would have became an exile from my tradition with periodic surges of nostalgia, particularly during the High Holidays and Passover. On entering the seminary I took upon myself the whole regimen of traditional Jewish practice, and I was pleased to discover that it was a freeing experience; I had the feeling of having returned home. There were still dark moments when I almost gave up the rabbinate, but without that commitment I might never have found my way back to a living Judaism.

With my prewar certainties gone, I searched the traditional sources for new understanding and in the process discovered that I didn't really understand much of what I already knew. From my studies in Poland I had retained knowledge of many texts, both biblical and Talmudic, but my understanding of these texts was clouded by the literalism that had dominated my education. In the yeshiva, history, philosophy, and even Hebrew grammar were not part of the curriculum; it was assumed that they would lead to heresy. My reeducation, which began at the university, took a positive turn at the seminary, where I approached the Jewish tradition with a minimum of preconceptions. The study of Jewish history introduced me to the varieties of Judaism that were practiced in different eras and places, as well as to its unifying themes, an experience that was both liberating and perplexing.

Eventually, I succeeded in freeing myself from the "all or nothing" thinking that characterized traditionalist polemics in prewar Poland and still does now. I realized that the "either/or" propositions about God and about Jewish observance were a trap, that the slippery slope is only for those who want to slide down. Most importantly, I learned that true religion is and always was complex, with faith and doubt intermingled. In this quest I found inspiration and support in the Bible itself. When Jeremiah turns to God and asks, "Why does the way of the wicked prosper? Why are the workers of treachery at ease?" (Jer. 12:1), he is asking the same question raised by all of us who are perplexed about the ways of God that are ultimately hidden from us.

As you would expect, the Book of Job played an important role in my reeducation. Here is a book that is part of sacred scripture, arguing against the accepted belief in divine reward and punishment. Job's friends, who represent the conventional view, try hard to persuade him that if he suffered he must have sinned, thus adding insult to injury. But Job, convinced that he is innocent, refuses to accept guilt. To this day I cringe when I hear that the Holocaust was a punishment for our sins. There is nothing more demeaning to Judaism than this crude and insensitive justification of the ways of God. The important lesson of Job is that despite what the Bible tells us about God, ultimately we do not know His ways. That is the significance of the questions that come at the end of the book. It is a sobering and humbling lesson, but one that befits human beings at all times.

Once the certainty of knowing the ways of God was gone, I had to learn to live with imponderables and paradoxes, with more questions than answers. Eventually I understood that questions, no matter how many and how cogent, are only questions. It is our impatience that turns them into answers. At the same time, I discovered that while the Bible and Talmud generally speak about God in positive and human terms, alongside them there are qualifications to warn us that we are dealing with metaphors. When the Bible tells us "Ki lo yirani ha'adam vahai" ("A person cannot see Me and live," Exod. 33:20), it is in effect telling us about the uniqueness and radical otherness of God.

After I had sufficiently freed myself from the literalism of my previous education, I realized that my conception of God was derived from a simplistic reading of traditional Jewish sources. It then occurred to me that my quarrels were not with God but with a particular conception of Him. Here I should say that what I had gained in understanding came at the cost of losing the comfort of a personal deity.

The next formidable task was dealing with the authority of the Torah. The sages of the Mishnah state that "Moses received the Torah from Sinai" (Avot 1:1). Here the word *Torah* includes the Bible and the oral tradition that was later committed to writing in the Talmud. Until modern times all Jews believed that both were divinely revealed. However, the application of literary, historical, philological, and archaeological tools to the study of the Bible showed that the biblical text is not uniform; that parts of it were from earlier and parts from later times; and that some biblical laws, narratives, and poetry were influenced by the literature of its neighbors. This raised the following question: If the Torah is not the word of God revealed to Moses, then what is its authority? Or, as an Orthodox Jew once asked me, "If you don't believe that the commandments were ordained by God, why would you bother to observe them?" My immediate response was, "Do you mean to say that unless God commanded our whole cultural-religious tradition, it's garbage?" Essentially what I was saying to this man was that the "either/or" approach to deciding the worth of a millennial cultural-religious tradition that inspired the creation of an extensive literature of law, philosophy, and mysticism, that sustained Jewish life in all parts of the globe, is too simplistic to be taken seriously.

After wrestling with this problem, I concluded that there is something wrong with a religious belief that requires us to ignore the accumulated evidence of learning that was acquired, not for the purpose of challenging God or the truth of Scripture, but in an effort to understand it. The idea of rejecting the findings of modern biblical scholarship to protect religious conceptions of the past is highly problematic.

Despite the persuasive arguments of modern scholarship, it wasn't easy for me to change my literalist belief about the Bible. But when this change finally occurred, it opened up new vistas. Whereas before I came to the Bible and Talmud with a set of beliefs that limited their meaning, now, with the help of modern scholarship I began to see their variety and richness. Believing that God verbally communicated the whole Torah to Moses certainly gives it authority, but such a belief requires seeing the Torah as a uniform text, which scholarship has shown that it is not. It leads to explaining away differing versions of laws and stories instead of accepting the fact that they derive from different periods and different sources. More to the point, it also leads to the notion of a "Judaism Eternal," a Judaism that has been the same ever since Sinai, whereas the Bible reports reforms that took place in the seventh century b.c.e. under King Josaiah, and the greatest reform of biblical religion was instituted by the rabbis of the Talmud. That reform resulted in the creation of Judaism, by which we have lived ever since.

Finally, the belief that the whole Torah was verbally revealed eliminates the cultural interplay between Jews and their neighbors that modern scholarship has recovered for us, an interplay that testifies to a creative Jewish religious civilization that was engaged in a give-and-take relationship with the surrounding nations. This fact, which is important in itself, also challenges the belief that Jews are a people apart from all other nations—an attitude that runs counter to historical facts. If the Jewish people had actually been insular and resistant to the ideas and beliefs of other cultures, we never would have had the flowering of medieval Jewish philosophy, poetry, ethics, and mysticism, much of it written in Arabic and influenced by the best thinking of the surrounding cultures, especially Islam.

In my wish to return to Jewish learning and living I wasn't concerned with the ultimate authority of the Torah, nor was I looking for an insurance policy on life in the world to come. What I was looking for was a way to return to my tradition. In my search I discovered that studying the Bible and Talmud and other traditional Jewish works was in itself an experience that led to practice, like the observance of Shabbat and holidays.

The knowledge that in the Holocaust human beings murdered other human beings whom they had never met before has never left me. Its frightening implication that "we" are potentially "they" is always with me. The antidote to this possibility is my reflection on the name *Israel*, which was given to the patriarch Jacob, "because he had striven with God and with people and had prevailed" (Gen. 32:29). Wrestling with God and with ourselves is an essential part of Jewish religious piety. This is particularly important in our time when some Jews, in their zeal for God, are prepared to suspend the ethical. As against that, what characterizes Judaism is the integration of the ritual and the ethical, the concern for both the holy and the human.

Houses of Study

A Jewish Woman among Books

By Ilana M. Blumberg

Set in "houses of study," from a Jewish grammar school and high school to a Jerusalem yeshiva for women to a secular American university, Illana M. Blumberg's memoir asks, in an intimate and poignant manner: what happens when the traditional Jewish ideal of learning asserts itself in a body that is female—a body directed by that same tradition toward a life of modesty, early marriage, and motherhood?

ISBN 0-8032-1367-0;
978-8032-1367-8 (cloth)

Holocaust Girls

History, Memory, and Other Obsessions

By S.L. Wisenberg

This bracing and vivid collection of essays gives voice to what some American Jews feel but don't express about their uneasy state of mind. These essays creatively and sometimes audaciously address the question of what it means to be an American Jew trying to negotiate overlapping identities—woman, writer, and urban intellectual in search of a moral way.

ISBN 0-8032-9866-8;
978-0-8032-9866-8 (paper)

Fat Boys

A Slim Book

By Sander L. Gilman

He is the epitome of health—or a walking time bomb. He is oversexed—or sexless. He is jolly—or hiding the tears of a clown. He is the picture of wealth and plenty—or the bloated, malnourished emblem of poverty. He is the fat man—a cultural icon, a social enigma, a pressing medical issue—and he is the subject of this remarkably rich book.

ISBN 0-8032-2183-5;
978-0-8032-2183-3 (cloth)